SUPPLY CHAIN MANAGEMENT

STRATEGIES FOR SUSTAINABILITY, AND RESILIENCE

AN EDITED BOOK

To all the visionaries and innovators who tirelessly work to enhance supply chain efficiency and transform global commerce.

And to the countless professionals and researchers who inspire collaboration and excellence in the field of supply chain management.

Contents

Foreword

In today's interconnected world, supply chain management stands as a cornerstone of global business success. The increasing complexity of modern markets, coupled with the ever-growing demand for efficiency, innovation, and sustainability, has transformed supply chain management from a background function into a strategic enabler.

This book delves into the intricacies of managing supply chains in dynamic environments, shedding light on the principles, challenges, and future trends of the field. By bridging theory and practice, it provides readers with actionable insights that are both profound and practical.

As industries evolve, the ability to adapt, optimize, and innovate in supply chain processes becomes more critical than ever. This work comes at a pivotal time, offering valuable perspectives that empower professionals, researchers, and leaders to tackle real-world challenges and seize new opportunities.
It is with great admiration and respect that I introduce this book to the global community of supply chain enthusiasts and practitioners. May it serve as a guide and inspiration for those who aim to navigate and shape the future of supply chain management.

Preface

Supply chain management has evolved into a pivotal function, driving value creation, innovation, and sustainability across industries. As businesses navigate an era marked by rapid technological advancements and global interconnectivity, mastering the art and science of supply chain management has become imperative for long-term success.

This book is born out of the desire to bridge the gap between theoretical frameworks and practical applications in the realm of supply chains. It provides a comprehensive exploration of strategies, challenges, and emerging trends, empowering readers to approach supply chain management with both confidence and creativity.

The content is designed for professionals, scholars, and students who seek to deepen their understanding of supply chain dynamics, while offering actionable insights that resonate in today's fast-paced, competitive landscape. Throughout the chapters, you will find real-world examples, case studies, and tools that illuminate the pathway to achieving supply chain excellence.

I hope this book will inspire readers to embrace innovation, foster collaboration, and lead with resilience in shaping the future of supply chains.

With gratitude to all contributors and supporters, this book reflects the collective effort and knowledge of the supply chain community. I trust it will serve as a valuable resource and a catalyst for growth.

Acknowledgements

This book is the result of collective efforts, guidance, and encouragement from many individuals and organizations.

I extend my heartfelt gratitude to my family, whose unwavering support and belief in my vision have been the foundation of my journey. Their patience and encouragement have been my source of strength throughout this endeavor.

I am deeply thankful to my mentors and colleagues, who have shared their invaluable knowledge and insights, shaping my understanding of supply chain management. Their constructive feedback and guidance have greatly enriched this work.

To the contributors, editors, and publishing team, I owe my thanks for their dedication, expertise, and relentless efforts in bringing this project to life.

Finally, I express my appreciation to all the professionals, researchers, and educators in the supply chain community, whose passion and commitment to excellence have inspired the ideas presented in this book.

This book is for all those who strive to make supply chains more innovative, efficient, and sustainable.

Prologue

The journey of supply chain management mirrors the evolution of commerce itself. From rudimentary trade systems to the intricate global networks that power today's economies, supply chains have always been at the heart of human progress. In an era dominated by technological breakthroughs and unprecedented challenges, the supply chain has transformed into a dynamic and strategic entity, shaping industries and impacting lives.

This book begins by exploring the essence of supply chain management—its roots, principles, and the forces driving its transformation. It aims to take readers on a voyage through the complexities of modern supply chains, providing insights into the innovative strategies that organizations employ to optimize operations and meet the demands of a fast-paced world.

The prologue sets the stage for a deeper understanding of how supply chains operate as ecosystems—interconnected, adaptive, and vital to global prosperity. It emphasizes the importance of collaboration, agility, and resilience in building systems that are not only efficient but also sustainable. As you turn the pages, you will discover the untapped potential of supply chain management, its role in reshaping industries, and its capacity to influence the future of commerce.

CHAPTER ONE

The Agile Supply Chain: Navigating Dynamics in a Changing World

Author: Dr. S. S. Chauhan, Assistant Professor at Sam Higginbottom University of Agriculture Technology & Sciences, Prayagraj, U.P

Abstract:

In an increasingly volatile and interconnected global market, supply chains must evolve to remain competitive and resilient. This chapter explores the concept of the Agile Supply Chain (ASC), emphasizing its ability to adapt swiftly to changing demands, market fluctuations, and unforeseen disruptions. Through a review of key principles and strategies, the chapter highlights how agile methodologies—originating from software development—have been successfully applied to supply chain management to enhance flexibility, responsiveness, and collaboration across various industries. The discussion includes the integration of real-time data, technology advancements, and cross-functional teamwork as crucial enablers of agility. By examining case studies and best practices, the chapter underscores the critical role of agility in managing uncertainty and driving innovation in supply chains. It also considers the challenges organizations face when implementing agile practices and offers insights into how they can overcome barriers to achieve a more adaptive and efficient supply chain model in a rapidly evolving business landscape.

Introduction

The modern business environment is characterized by volatility, uncertainty, complexity, and ambiguity (VUCA). Traditional supply chain models, driven by cost minimization and standardization, have proven insufficient in addressing rapid market shifts. The Agile Supply Chain model has emerged as a transformative framework designed to enable responsiveness, flexibility, and resilience.

This chapter explores the concept, principles, and implementation strategies of agile supply chains while analyzing real-world applications that ensure organizations remain competitive amidst evolving market demands.

Defining Agile Supply Chain

An agile supply chain is designed to thrive in uncertainty. It refers to an organization's capability to swiftly and effectively adjust supply chain configurations, operations, and strategies in response to dynamic market conditions, disruptions, or shifts in customer demand. Unlike traditional supply chains that focus primarily on cost efficiency and stability, agile supply chains prioritize speed, flexibility, and adaptability to gain a competitive edge in volatile environments.

Key Characteristics:

- **Flexibility:** Agile supply chains can reconfigure sourcing, production, and distribution strategies quickly. Whether it's switching suppliers, adjusting product lines, or rerouting logistics, flexibility enables businesses to manage risk and seize new opportunities with minimal disruption.

- **Responsiveness:** Responsiveness is the ability to sense changes—such as market demand spikes, supply shortages, or geopolitical events—and react promptly. Agile systems leverage real-time data and predictive analytics to drive faster, more informed decision-making across the supply chain.

- **Collaboration:** Strong, trust-based partnerships across suppliers, manufacturers, logistics providers, and retailers are vital. Collaboration ensures timely and accurate information sharing, aligned objectives, and coordinated responses to challenges, leading to improved resilience and performance.

- **Customer-Centricity:** At the heart of agility is the end customer. Agile supply chains are designed to deliver greater value by being more responsive to customer preferences, customization needs, and service expectations. This focus helps build loyalty and competitive differentiation.

Core Principles of Agile Supply Chain

1. **Market Sensitivity:** Agile supply chains are highly responsive to market changes, enabled by real-time data analytics. This principle emphasizes understanding customer demand patterns, preferences, and shifts by closely monitoring point-of-sale data, social media trends, and other dynamic market indicators. The goal is to sense and respond quickly to changes, minimizing delays and overstock or understock issues.
2. **Virtual Integration:** This principle focuses on creating seamless information flows across the supply chain using advanced digital technologies. Cloud-based platforms, IoT sensors, and blockchain enable transparency, real-time tracking, and secure data sharing among partners. Virtual integration helps companies make informed decisions, reduce lead times, and improve overall operational efficiency.
3. **Process Integration:** Agility requires end-to-end collaboration. This involves synchronized planning, shared goals, and open communication between suppliers, manufacturers, logistics providers, and even customers. Integrated processes ensure faster response times, reduce errors, and create a unified approach to handling disruptions or sudden demand surges.
4. **Network Flexibility:** An agile supply chain is designed to adapt. By building diverse supplier bases, maintaining dual sourcing strategies, and establishing responsive logistics networks, companies can pivot quickly when disruptions occur. Flexibility also means being able to scale operations up or down based on real-time demand, thereby improving resilience and service continuity.

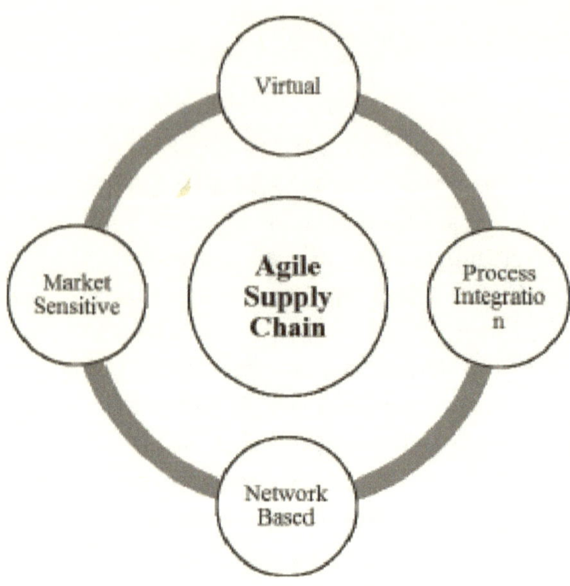

Core Principles of Agile Supply Chain

Strategies for Building an Agile Supply Chain

To build an agile supply chain, organizations must adopt a holistic and proactive approach that balances speed, flexibility, and resilience. One of the foundational strategies is investing in real-time data and advanced analytics. By leveraging technologies such as AI, machine learning, and IoT, companies can gain end-to-end visibility across their supply chain, enabling faster, data-driven decisions and early detection of disruptions. Equally important is fostering strong collaboration across the value chain—working closely with suppliers, logistics providers, and customers to ensure seamless information sharing and synchronized operations. This collaborative environment can be supported by integrated digital platforms and shared forecasting tools. Additionally, designing the supply chain to be modular and flexible allows businesses to reconfigure sourcing, production, and distribution rapidly in response to market changes or supply interruptions. Embracing automation and digitization also plays a crucial role in boosting operational efficiency and agility; robotic process automation (RPA), smart warehousing, and cloud-based systems streamline workflows and reduce manual dependencies. Beyond technology, building a culture of agility within the workforce is essential. Cross-functional teams trained in agile principles and empowered to make quick decisions can greatly enhance the organization's responsiveness. Risk management and scenario planning further strengthen agility by preparing the organization for potential disruptions, enabling faster and more coordinated responses. Finally, customer-centricity must be at the core of all strategies—agile supply chains must be designed to meet changing consumer preferences, ensure timely deliveries, and support personalized experiences. Together, these strategies form a resilient, responsive, and future-ready supply chain capable of thriving in an increasingly dynamic and uncertain world.

1. Technological Advancements:

- Use of AI for demand forecasting and scenario planning.
- Implementation of automation for increased production agility.
- Adoption of blockchain for secure and transparent transactions.

2. Dynamic Workforce Allocation:

- Training employees to multitask and adapt to various roles within the supply chain.
- Remote working solutions for supply chain managers and coordinators.

3. Supplier Collaboration and Risk Sharing:

- Joint ventures for resource pooling.
- Contracts emphasizing shared risks and rewards.

4. Demand-Driven Models:

- Integration of just-in-time (JIT) principles.
- Real-time tracking and inventory management systems.

Benefits and Challenges

Benefits:

- Improved customer satisfaction through faster deliveries.
- Enhanced resilience against disruptions.
- Higher adaptability to new product launches or market entry.

Challenges:

- Initial high cost of implementing technologies.
- Complexity in coordinating diverse stakeholders.
- Need for cultural change within the organization.

Case Studies: Real-World Applications of Agile Supply Chains

1. Zara: Agile Fashion Through Localized Production and Real-Time Insights

Zara, a flagship brand of Inditex, has become a global benchmark for agility in the fashion industry. The company revolutionized supply chain responsiveness by localizing a significant portion of its production in Europe, particularly Spain, allowing for shorter lead times and faster turnaround from design to store shelves.

Key agility strategies:

- **Real-Time Inventory Management:** Zara uses a highly digitized system to track sales data daily, which informs design and replenishment decisions almost instantly.
- **Fast Design-to-Delivery Cycle:** New fashion items can be designed, produced, and delivered to stores within just 2–3 weeks, compared to the industry norm of several months.
- **Frequent Product Refreshes:** Limited production runs create a sense of urgency for consumers and allow Zara to continuously adapt its offerings to real-time fashion trends.

2. Amazon: Tech-Driven Agility in Last-Mile Logistics

Amazon exemplifies agility at scale, particularly in last-mile delivery, where speed, efficiency, and flexibility are critical. The company leverages advanced technologies and a decentralized fulfillment model to meet rapidly shifting customer expectations.

Key agility strategies:

- **Robotics and Automation:** Amazon's fulfillment centers use robotic systems to sort, pick, and move products, increasing speed and reducing processing errors.
- **AI-Powered Demand Forecasting:** Machine learning algorithms anticipate what products will be needed and where, enabling pre-

positioning of inventory.

- **Dynamic Delivery Networks:** Through Amazon Flex and its vast transportation ecosystem, the company adjusts delivery routes in real-time, optimizing for speed and cost.

3. Procter & Gamble (P&G): Hybrid Supply Chain for Resilience and Responsiveness

Procter & Gamble balances agility with operational efficiency through a hybrid supply chain model, which combines centralized manufacturing for scale and cost-efficiency with decentralized capabilities for responsiveness.

Key agility strategies:

- **Smart Factories:** P&G has adopted Industry 4.0 technologies, including IoT sensors and predictive maintenance, to increase agility in production.
- **Dual Sourcing and Regional Hubs:** The company uses multiple suppliers and strategically located manufacturing facilities to ensure continuity and adaptability during disruptions.
- **Customer-Centric Planning:** P&G works closely with retail partners, using POS data and collaborative forecasting to align supply with actual demand.

Future Trends in Agile Supply Chain

As global markets become increasingly volatile and consumer expectations evolve, supply chains must continue to innovate and transform. The future of agile supply chains lies at the intersection of technology, sustainability, and resilience, enabling organizations to not only respond swiftly to change but also proactively shape it.

Hyper-Automation: Hyper-automation refers to the end-to-end automation of processes using a combination of advanced technologies such as Artificial Intelligence (AI), Robotic Process Automation (RPA), Machine Learning (ML), and digital twins.

Key impacts:

- **Predictive Decision-Making:** AI and ML models can forecast demand shifts, detect anomalies, and optimize inventory more accurately than traditional methods.

- **Smart Warehousing:** Automated picking, packing, and sorting systems reduce human error and accelerate order fulfillment.
- **Seamless Operations:** RPA streamlines routine tasks like invoice processing, order tracking, and compliance reporting, freeing up human workers for strategic roles.

This trend allows for faster, more informed decisions, especially in high-volume, high-variability environments.

Circular Supply Chains:

In contrast to the traditional linear model (produce-use-dispose), circular supply chains focus on sustainability, minimizing environmental impact while maintaining operational agility.

Key components:

- **Product Lifecycle Extension:** Designing products for reuse, refurbishment, or recycling.
- **Reverse Logistics:** Efficiently managing returns and reintroducing materials back into the production cycle.
- **Eco-Friendly Sourcing:** Partnering with suppliers that prioritize sustainable practices and materials.

Circular supply chains not only meet rising consumer and regulatory demands for environmental responsibility but also improve resource efficiency and cost savings in the long term.

Resilient Ecosystems:

The COVID-19 pandemic, geopolitical tensions, and natural disasters have underscored the need for resilient supply chains that can withstand and quickly recover from disruptions.

Key features:

- **Multi-Tier Visibility:** Real-time monitoring of not just direct suppliers, but also second- and third-tier partners to identify potential risks early.
- **Scenario Planning & Risk Mapping:** Leveraging AI to model disruption scenarios and pre-define response strategies.
- **Decentralized Operations:** Diversifying suppliers and logistics partners across regions to reduce dependency on single sources.

By building resilient ecosystems, companies gain the agility to pivot during crises and maintain continuity under pressure.

Conclusion

The Agile Supply Chain is no longer a competitive advantage but a necessity in the fast-evolving global economy. Businesses must embrace innovation, foster collaboration, and integrate robust digital tools to thrive. Organizations that effectively implement agile strategies will position themselves for sustained success.

CHAPTER TWO

Blockchain in Supply Chain: Revolutionizing Transparency and Efficiency

Author: Dr. Pradeep Munda, Assistant Professor at BIT Mesra, Ranchi, Jharkhand

Abstract:

Blockchain technology is transforming traditional supply chain models by enhancing transparency, traceability, and operational efficiency. This chapter explores the growing role of blockchain in supply chain management, focusing on its potential to address long-standing challenges such as counterfeiting, fraud, inefficiencies, and lack of trust between stakeholders. By providing a decentralized and immutable ledger, blockchain ensures that every transaction and movement of goods is recorded transparently and securely, allowing real-time tracking and verification. The chapter delves into various applications of blockchain across different supply chain stages, from procurement to delivery, highlighting the benefits of reducing delays, improving accuracy, and fostering collaboration. Additionally, the chapter discusses the technical and operational challenges associated with blockchain adoption, including scalability, integration with existing systems, and regulatory concerns. Through case studies and examples, the chapter demonstrates how blockchain is revolutionizing supply chains by fostering greater trust and enabling more efficient, secure, and sustainable business practices.

Introduction

The traditional supply chain landscape often faces challenges of inefficiency, lack of transparency, and trust among stakeholders. Blockchain technology has emerged as a groundbreaking solution, offering a decentralized and tamper-proof platform that redefines how supply chains operate. This chapter explores the principles of blockchain technology and its transformative potential in supply chain management.

Understanding Blockchain Technology

Blockchain technology is fundamentally a decentralized, distributed ledger system that records and stores data across a network of computers, or nodes, in a way that ensures transparency, security, and immutability. Unlike traditional centralized databases, blockchain operates on a peer-to-peer architecture where each transaction is time-stamped, encrypted, and linked to the previous one, forming a chain of blocks that cannot be altered retroactively without consensus from the network. This feature makes blockchain particularly powerful for ensuring data integrity and trust among multiple stakeholders who may not fully trust each other. In the context of supply chain management, blockchain enhances visibility by providing a single source of truth that all parties can access in real-time, enabling seamless traceability of products from origin to destination. It can also reduce fraud, streamline compliance, automate processes through smart contracts, and improve overall efficiency by eliminating intermediaries. By fostering accountability and transparency at every stage of the supply chain, blockchain empowers organizations to respond more quickly to disruptions, build consumer trust, and support sustainable and ethical sourcing practices.

Key Features of Blockchain:

- **Decentralized Network:** A decentralized network is one of the defining characteristics of blockchain technology, setting it apart from traditional centralized systems. In a centralized model, all data and decision-making power are controlled by a single authority or server, making the system vulnerable to failures, cyberattacks, or manipulation. Blockchain, in contrast, operates through a distributed network of nodes—each of which holds a copy of the entire ledger and participates in validating and recording transactions. This decentralization eliminates the need for a central authority, reducing bottlenecks and the risk of a single point of failure. It enhances trust among participants, as no single entity can unilaterally alter the records. Moreover, decentralization fosters greater system resilience, transparency, and democratic participation, as all nodes have equal access to information and contribute to maintaining the integrity of the network. This makes blockchain particularly valuable in multi-party ecosystems like supply chains, finance, and governance, where trust, data consistency, and fault tolerance are critical.

- **Immutability:** Immutability is a core feature of blockchain technology that ensures once data is recorded on the blockchain, it cannot be altered, deleted, or tampered with. Each transaction is encrypted and linked to the previous one, forming a chronological chain of blocks secured by cryptographic hashes. Any attempt to change a single block would require altering all subsequent blocks across the entire network—a computationally infeasible task without majority consensus. This permanent and tamper-proof nature of blockchain records guarantees data integrity, making it a trusted source of truth in environments where accuracy and reliability are critical. For instance, in supply chains, immutability ensures that records related to sourcing, production, and delivery cannot be falsified, thus preventing fraud and enhancing traceability. It also supports auditability, as stakeholders can verify historical data at any time without the risk of discrepancies. Overall, immutability reinforces transparency and accountability, building trust among all participants in the blockchain ecosystem.

- **Smart Contracts:** Smart contracts are self-executing digital agreements embedded within the blockchain, where the terms and conditions are directly written into code. These contracts automatically trigger and enforce actions—such as releasing payments, updating records, or approving transactions—once predefined conditions are met, without the need for intermediaries. This automation reduces the risk of human error, fraud, and delays, while also lowering administrative costs. Smart contracts operate with transparency and reliability, as all stakeholders can view the terms and outcomes, and once deployed, they cannot be altered without network consensus. In supply chain applications, for example, a smart contract can automatically initiate payment to a supplier once goods are delivered and verified by a sensor-enabled tracking system. Similarly, in insurance, claims can be processed instantly when qualifying events are validated through external data feeds. By streamlining processes and ensuring tamper-proof execution, smart contracts add a layer of efficiency, trust, and enforceability to blockchain-based ecosystems.

- **Transparency:** Transparency is a key advantage of blockchain technology, referring to the open visibility of data across the network through a shared, distributed ledger. In blockchain systems, all validated transactions are recorded chronologically and are accessible in real time to authorized stakeholders. This means that every participant in the network can view the same information, fostering a sense of trust and accountability. Unlike traditional systems where data may be siloed or controlled by a single entity, blockchain's transparency ensures that no participant can manipulate records without it being immediately evident to others. This feature is particularly valuable in multi-party processes such as supply chains, where manufacturers, suppliers, logistics providers, and retailers can all track the movement and status of goods with a single, unified view. Real-time access to accurate data enhances decision-making, simplifies audits, reduces disputes, and supports compliance with regulatory standards. Importantly, while blockchain promotes transparency, it also respects data privacy by allowing access control through permissions, ensuring that sensitive information is only visible to those with the appropriate authorization.

Applications of Blockchain in Supply Chain

- **Enhanced Traceability and Transparency:** Enhanced traceability and transparency are among the most impactful benefits that blockchain technology brings to modern supply chains. By leveraging a decentralized, tamper-proof ledger, blockchain enables end-to-end visibility across all stages of the product lifecycle—from raw material sourcing to manufacturing, distribution, and final delivery to the customer. Every transaction or event is time-stamped and recorded in real time, creating a permanent, verifiable audit trail that stakeholders can access at any point. This level of traceability allows businesses to pinpoint the exact location and condition of goods, verify the authenticity of products, and quickly identify the source of any issues or disruptions. For example, in the food and pharmaceutical industries, blockchain can be used to trace contaminated products back to their origin within seconds, enabling faster recalls and minimizing health risks. At the same time, transparency ensures that all authorized participants—such as suppliers, regulators, and consumers—have shared access to accurate and up-to-date information, fostering trust, accountability, and ethical business practices. This not only enhances operational efficiency but also strengthens brand reputation and regulatory compliance.

- ○ **Example:** Walmart uses blockchain to trace the origin of food products, reducing contamination risks.

- **Improved Trust Among Stakeholders:** Improved trust among stakeholders is a significant outcome of implementing blockchain technology, particularly in complex, multi-party ecosystems like supply chains. Because blockchain maintains a transparent, immutable, and verifiable ledger, it ensures that every transaction and data entry is visible to authorized participants and cannot be altered without consensus. This openness fosters a culture of accountability and integrity, reducing disputes and building confidence among suppliers, manufacturers, distributors, and even end consumers. Stakeholders no longer need to rely solely on intermediaries or third-party verifications, as the blockchain itself serves as a single source of truth. For example, suppliers can trust that payments will be made as agreed once conditions are met through smart contracts; manufacturers can confirm the authenticity of raw materials; and consumers can trace the origins of the products they purchase, ensuring ethical sourcing and quality standards. In essence, blockchain bridges trust gaps, enabling smoother collaboration, stronger partnerships, and more resilient, transparent supply chain networks.
- **Fraud Prevention:** Fraud prevention is one of the most compelling advantages of blockchain technology, driven by its inherent features of immutability and transparency. Once data is recorded on the blockchain, it becomes permanent and tamper-proof, meaning it cannot be altered, deleted, or backdated without consensus from the entire network. This creates a secure and trustworthy record of every transaction, significantly reducing opportunities for data manipulation, forgery, or counterfeiting. In supply chains, this is particularly valuable for verifying the authenticity of products, especially in industries vulnerable to fraud such as pharmaceuticals, luxury goods, electronics, and food. For instance, each product can be tagged with a unique identifier linked to blockchain entries that document its origin, manufacturing process, and journey through the supply chain. Any attempt to insert counterfeit

goods or falsify information is immediately detectable, as discrepancies cannot be hidden from the shared ledger. By making fraudulent activity not only difficult but also easily traceable, blockchain technology strengthens regulatory compliance, brand integrity, and consumer protection, while also reducing the cost of fraud-related investigations and losses.

- ◦ **Example:** The pharmaceutical industry leverages blockchain to ensure the authenticity of drugs.

- **Supply Chain Automation :** Supply chain automation is significantly enhanced by the use of smart contracts within blockchain technology. Smart contracts are self-executing agreements with predefined rules and conditions coded directly into the blockchain. When these conditions are met—such as the successful delivery of goods or verification of quality—the contract automatically triggers the corresponding action, such as releasing payment, updating inventory records, or notifying stakeholders. This removes the need for manual intervention or third-party mediation, thereby streamlining operations, reducing administrative costs, and minimizing delays. For example, once a shipment reaches its destination and is confirmed via IoT-enabled sensors or digital signatures, a smart contract can instantly initiate payment to the supplier, ensuring faster and more reliable transactions. This level of automation enhances operational efficiency, increases trust between trading partners, and allows for more agile, responsive supply chains. Furthermore, by eliminating bottlenecks and reducing paperwork, smart contracts contribute to a more scalable and resilient supply chain infrastructure.

- **Sustainability and Ethical Sourcing :** Supply chain automation is significantly enhanced by the use of smart contracts within blockchain technology. Smart contracts are self-executing agreements with predefined rules and conditions coded directly into the blockchain. When these conditions are met—such as the successful delivery of goods or verification of quality—the contract automatically triggers the corresponding action, such as releasing payment, updating inventory records, or notifying stakeholders. This removes the need for manual intervention or third-party mediation, thereby streamlining operations, reducing administrative costs, and minimizing delays. For example, once a shipment reaches its destination and is confirmed via IoT-enabled sensors or digital signatures, a smart contract can instantly initiate payment to the supplier, ensuring faster and more reliable transactions. This level of automation enhances operational efficiency, increases trust between trading partners, and allows for more agile, responsive supply chains. Furthermore, by eliminating bottlenecks and reducing paperwork, smart contracts contribute to a more scalable and resilient supply chain infrastructure.

Challenges in Blockchain Adoption Despite its promising advantages, blockchain adoption faces several significant challenges that organizations must carefully navigate. One of the primary obstacles is scalability—as the number of transactions increases, many blockchain platforms struggle with processing speed and energy efficiency, making it difficult to implement at large scale. Additionally, integration with existing systems can be complex and costly, especially for legacy infrastructure that lacks compatibility with blockchain architecture. Regulatory uncertainty also poses a barrier, as global standards for blockchain governance, data privacy, and cross-border transactions are still evolving. Moreover, the lack of technical expertise and skilled professionals in blockchain development hinders adoption, particularly for small to mid-sized enterprises. Data privacy concerns may arise in permissionless or public blockchains where sensitive business information could potentially be exposed. Finally, building trust among stakeholders in a decentralized system—ironically, one of blockchain's strengths—can be challenging, especially in industries where participants are accustomed to centralized control. Addressing these challenges requires a combination of technological innovation, regulatory clarity, industry collaboration, and investment in education and training to fully unlock blockchain's potential.

- **High Implementation Costs:**

  - One of the most significant barriers to adopting blockchain technology is the high implementation cost associated with its development, integration, and maintenance. Building a blockchain-based system from the ground up requires substantial investment in specialized hardware, software, and infrastructure, as well as skilled technical expertise—all of which come at a premium. Additionally, integrating blockchain with existing enterprise systems, such as ERP or supply chain management platforms, can be complex and resource-intensive, often requiring custom development and process redesign. The costs are further compounded by the need for ongoing maintenance, cybersecurity, compliance, and training programs to ensure successful long-term adoption. For many small and medium-sized enterprises (SMEs), these financial and technical demands can be prohibitive, limiting blockchain deployment to larger organizations with greater budgets and IT capabilities. As the technology matures and more scalable, user-friendly platforms emerge, the hope is that implementation costs will decrease, making blockchain more accessible across industries and business sizes.

- **Scalability Issues:**

  - Scalability remains a critical challenge in the widespread adoption of blockchain technology, particularly when it comes to handling large volumes of transactions efficiently. Most traditional blockchain networks, such as Bitcoin and Ethereum, operate on consensus mechanisms like Proof of Work (PoW), which, while secure, are computationally intensive and relatively slow. As a result, these networks can only process a limited number of transactions per second compared to conventional centralized systems like Visa or PayPal. This limitation leads to congestion, increased transaction times, and higher processing fees when the network becomes saturated. In a fast-paced environment like supply chain management—where real-time data exchange, rapid decision-making, and high throughput are crucial—such bottlenecks can hinder operational efficiency. Although newer consensus mechanisms like Proof of Stake (PoS), sharding, and Layer 2 solutions are being developed to address these limitations, achieving true scalability without compromising security and decentralization remains a complex technical hurdle. Solving scalability issues is essential for blockchain to support large-scale, enterprise-level applications across global networks.

- **Data Privacy Concerns:**

- ◦ Data privacy concerns are a significant challenge in the adoption of blockchain technology, especially as organizations strive to balance transparency with the protection of sensitive information. One of blockchain's core strengths—its transparent and immutable ledger—can become a double-edged sword when it comes to storing or sharing confidential data. In public or permissionless blockchains, all transactions are visible to all participants, which could expose proprietary business information, trade secrets, or personal customer data. Even in private or consortium blockchains, where access is restricted, there are still concerns about how much data should be visible to different parties. These challenges are further complicated by regulations such as GDPR, which require the ability to modify or delete personal data—something inherently difficult, if not impossible, on an immutable ledger. To address these concerns, blockchain systems must incorporate robust privacy-preserving technologies such as zero-knowledge proofs, encryption, off-chain data storage, and permissioned access layers. Striking the right balance between openness and confidentiality is essential to ensuring compliance, building trust, and enabling responsible blockchain adoption across data-sensitive industries like healthcare, finance, and supply chain management.

- **Lack of Standardization:**

  - ◦ The lack of standardization is a critical obstacle hindering the seamless adoption and integration of blockchain technology across industries. As blockchain is still an emerging field, there is currently no universally accepted set of protocols, data formats, or interoperability guidelines, leading to a fragmented ecosystem of platforms and solutions that often cannot communicate effectively with one another. This fragmentation makes it difficult for businesses to integrate blockchain into their existing systems or collaborate across supply chains, particularly when different stakeholders use incompatible technologies. Additionally, the absence of standard compliance frameworks can create uncertainty around legal enforceability, data governance, and cross-border transactions. Without clear and consistent standards, organizations face increased complexity, risk, and cost when deploying blockchain solutions, particularly at scale. Standardization is essential not only for interoperability and scalability, but also for building trust and ensuring compliance with regulations. As industry bodies and international organizations begin to develop unified blockchain standards, greater alignment is expected to drive more widespread and effective adoption.

Case Studies

- **Maersk & IBM's TradeLens Platform:**

  - Maersk & IBM's TradeLens platform is a pioneering example of blockchain technology transforming the global shipping industry. Launched as a joint venture, TradeLens was designed to address the longstanding inefficiencies in international trade by providing a secure, transparent, and tamper-proof digital ecosystem for all parties involved in the supply chain. Using blockchain as its foundation, the platform enables real-time sharing of shipping data and documents—such as bills of lading, customs clearances, and cargo status—among a global network of shippers, freight forwarders, ports, customs authorities, and ocean carriers. This drastically reduces the need for manual paperwork, mitigates the risk of fraud, and improves operational efficiency. TradeLens not only enhances end-to-end visibility and trust among stakeholders, but also streamlines cross-border transactions by automating key workflows through smart contracts. By digitizing and securing traditionally paper-heavy processes, the platform has demonstrated how blockchain can revolutionize transparency, traceability, and speed in global logistics. While TradeLens officially ceased operations in 2023 due to market adoption challenges, it remains a valuable case study in how blockchain can reimagine the future of global trade and inspire more collaborative, tech-driven solutions.

- **Provenance:**

  - Provenance is an innovative platform that leverages blockchain technology to verify and communicate the ethical and sustainable origins of food, fashion, and consumer products. By using blockchain's immutable ledger, Provenance allows brands to securely record and share key data points about a product's journey—from raw material sourcing and production to distribution and retail. Each step is time-stamped and verifiable, providing consumers with transparent access to information such as where, how, and by whom a product was made. This is particularly valuable in industries where environmental impact, labor practices, and authenticity are major consumer concerns. For example, Provenance has partnered with brands to trace organic cotton in fashion or fair-trade ingredients in food products, ensuring that ethical claims are substantiated by verifiable data rather than marketing rhetoric. Through blockchain-enabled QR codes or digital passports, shoppers can scan a product and instantly see its verified supply chain story. By empowering ethical consumption and promoting brand accountability, Provenance demonstrates how blockchain can build trust, support sustainability, and drive positive change in global supply networks.

- **Everledger:**

  - Everledger is a leading blockchain-based platform that aims to combat fraud, reduce theft, and ensure ethical sourcing within the diamond industry by providing a secure digital record of a diamond's provenance. Each diamond registered on Everledger's platform is assigned a unique digital identity that includes over 40 metadata points, such as color, cut, carat, clarity, and serial number—verified through high-resolution imaging and certification. This information is immutably recorded on the blockchain, creating a tamper-proof and transparent ledger that tracks the diamond's journey from mine to market. By making this data accessible to manufacturers, retailers, insurers, and consumers, Everledger helps prevent the circulation of conflict diamonds and counterfeit gems, while also streamlining verification for insurance and resale purposes. Consumers, in turn, gain greater confidence in the authenticity and ethical sourcing of their purchases. Beyond diamonds, Everledger has expanded its technology to other high-value goods like wine, art, and luxury watches, showcasing the versatility of blockchain in enhancing trust and traceability across complex value chains.

Future Trends and Opportunities

- **Integration with IoT:**

  - Integration with IoT (Internet of Things) devices significantly enhances the power of blockchain in supply chain operations by enabling real-time tracking, monitoring, and automated data collection. IoT devices such as GPS trackers, RFID tags, temperature sensors, and smart containers can be embedded throughout the supply chain to continuously capture critical data—such as location, temperature, humidity, and handling conditions of goods. When this data is recorded directly onto a blockchain, it becomes immutable and verifiable, ensuring transparency and accountability across all stages of the supply chain. For instance, in the pharmaceutical or food industries, blockchain-IoT integration can confirm that temperature-sensitive products have been stored and transported within the required thresholds, reducing the risk of spoilage or regulatory non-compliance. Moreover, this integration enables automated alerts and smart contract execution, such as triggering payments upon delivery or initiating action if a shipment deviates from predefined parameters. The result is a more responsive, secure, and intelligent supply chain ecosystem, where stakeholders can make informed decisions quickly and confidently based on trusted, real-time data.

- **Blockchain-as-a-Service (BaaS):**

  - Blockchain-as-a-Service (BaaS) is a cloud-based solution that allows businesses to build, host, and deploy their own blockchain applications without having to manage the complex infrastructure typically required. Offered by major tech providers like Microsoft (Azure), Amazon (AWS), IBM, and Oracle, BaaS platforms simplify the adoption of blockchain technology by providing preconfigured environments, developer tools, and integration support. This model is especially beneficial for companies that want to experiment with blockchain or incorporate it into their operations without incurring the high costs and technical barriers of developing solutions from scratch. BaaS platforms handle backend operations such as network setup, security, scalability, compliance, and updates, allowing organizations to focus on building use cases tailored to their industry needs—whether it's supply chain tracking, identity management, smart contract deployment, or digital asset management. By lowering the entry threshold, BaaS is accelerating mainstream blockchain adoption, making it accessible to businesses of all sizes and across diverse sectors, from logistics and finance to healthcare and retail.

- **Interoperability Solutions:**

  - Interoperability solutions are critical for the next phase of blockchain adoption, aiming to enable seamless communication and data exchange between different blockchain networks. As the blockchain ecosystem grows, numerous platforms—such as Ethereum, Hyperledger, Solana, and Polkadot—operate in silos with varying architectures, consensus mechanisms, and smart contract languages. This fragmentation limits cross-chain functionality and creates inefficiencies in multi-platform environments. Interoperability solutions seek to overcome this by developing standardized protocols, APIs, and bridges that allow blockchains to share information, transfer digital assets, and execute cross-chain smart contracts securely. Leading projects like Polkadot, Cosmos, and Quant's Overledger are at the forefront of this movement, building frameworks that connect public and private blockchains alike. In supply chain contexts, interoperability ensures that data from different vendors, logistics providers, or platforms can be integrated and verified across the entire value chain—regardless of the underlying blockchain being used. This facilitates greater collaboration, scalability, and efficiency, and paves the way for a truly interconnected and decentralized digital economy.

- **Sustainability Initiatives:**

  - Blockchain technology is playing an increasingly vital role in sustainability initiatives by enabling transparent and verifiable tracking of carbon emissions and environmental impact across supply chains. With growing consumer and regulatory pressure for greener operations, companies are turning to blockchain to track and report their carbon footprints, waste generation, water usage, and other key sustainability metrics in real time. By leveraging blockchain's immutable ledger, businesses can record sustainability-related data at each stage of the supply chain—from raw material extraction to production, transportation, and end-of-life recycling. This provides a reliable and auditable trail that can be shared with stakeholders, regulators, and eco-conscious consumers. Additionally, blockchain supports the use of tokenized carbon credits and green certifications, allowing organizations to offset emissions or prove compliance with environmental standards. Platforms like IBM's Green Horizon and ClimateChain are already enabling companies to validate eco-friendly claims, prevent greenwashing, and incentivize sustainable practices. As blockchain and IoT converge, supply chains are becoming not only more efficient but also more accountable and environmentally responsible.

Conclusion

Blockchain technology is revolutionizing supply chain management by fostering transparency, trust, and efficiency. Despite challenges, its potential to address longstanding issues in global supply chains makes it an indispensable tool for the future. Businesses must embrace collaboration and innovation to fully leverage blockchain's transformative power.

CHAPTER THREE

Mitigating Financial Risk in Nepalese banking

Author: Belal Ahmad, Branch Manager at Nepal Investment Mega Bank Limited

Abstract:

The Nepalese banking sector, like many others globally, faces significant challenges in managing financial risk, particularly in light of evolving economic conditions, regulatory changes, and regional uncertainties. This chapter examines the key financial risks encountered by banks in Nepal, including credit risk, market risk, liquidity risk, and operational risk. It explores the strategies and tools employed by Nepalese banks to mitigate these risks, with a focus on risk assessment frameworks, the role of regulatory bodies, and the implementation of risk management practices in alignment with international standards. Through a detailed analysis of recent trends, case studies, and emerging risk factors, the chapter highlights how banks in Nepal are leveraging technology, strengthening internal controls, and enhancing financial literacy to improve their risk management processes. Additionally, it addresses the challenges unique to the Nepalese context, such as limited access to financial data, political instability, and the relatively underdeveloped financial market infrastructure. The chapter concludes with recommendations for improving financial risk mitigation in Nepalese banking, emphasizing the importance of regulatory reforms, capacity building, and the adoption of innovative financial technologies.

Introduction

Financial risk is a significant concern in Nepalese banking, particularly in the context of supply chain management (SCM). The integration of financial institutions with supply chains enables businesses to ensure liquidity, optimize cash flow, and manage working capital efficiently. However, various financial risks such as credit risk, liquidity risk, operational risk, and regulatory risk pose challenges to the smooth functioning of supply chain networks. This chapter explores the financial risks in Nepalese banking related to SCM and discusses strategies for mitigating these risks.

Financial Risks in Nepalese Banking for SCM

1. **Credit Risk** Credit risk refers to the possibility that suppliers or buyers may default on their financial obligations, such as delayed payments or complete non-fulfillment of dues. In the context of Nepal, this risk is amplified by several structural and economic challenges. The country's economic volatility—driven by political instability, inflation, and fluctuating trade conditions—creates uncertainty in financial transactions across the supply chain. Moreover, the lack of robust credit assessment systems and limited access to reliable financial data make it difficult for businesses to accurately evaluate the creditworthiness of their partners. Many small and medium enterprises (SMEs) in Nepal operate informally, with inadequate documentation or financial history, further complicating credit risk evaluation. Additionally, the absence of widespread credit insurance and underdeveloped financial institutions limits risk mitigation options. As a result, businesses often operate under conservative terms or with limited trust, hindering supply chain fluidity and collaboration. Addressing credit risk in Nepal will require a combination of financial literacy, digital record-keeping, credit scoring innovations, and greater institutional support to foster a more transparent and secure trade environment.

2. **Liquidity Risk** Liquidity risk arises when supply chain participants face difficulties in accessing sufficient cash or credit to meet their short-term financial obligations. In Nepal, this risk is particularly pronounced due to liquidity constraints within the banking sector, which can hinder the timely disbursement of loans and credit lines essential for day-to-day operations. Many businesses in the supply chain, especially SMEs, depend heavily on short-term financing to cover operational expenses like inventory procurement, transportation, and wage payments. However, delays in payments from buyers, irregular cash flow cycles, and a lack of diversified funding sources often strain their working

capital. Compounding this issue are regulatory restrictions on liquidity management, including tight monetary policies and limited access to capital markets. Additionally, bureaucratic hurdles, lengthy loan approval processes, and risk-averse lending practices by financial institutions create bottlenecks in credit access. As a result, even financially viable businesses may struggle to maintain smooth operations, leading to disruptions across the supply chain. Tackling liquidity risk in Nepal requires improved financial infrastructure, greater access to digital financing tools, and supportive policies that enhance credit availability, transparency, and resilience in supply chain financing.

3. **Operational Risk** Operational risk refers to the potential for losses resulting from inadequate or failed internal processes, human error, fraud, cyber threats, or technological malfunctions. In Nepal, these risks are magnified by systemic and infrastructural limitations, particularly in the financial and banking sectors that support supply chain activities. Many organizations still rely on manual processes and outdated technologies, which increases the likelihood of data entry errors, delayed transactions, and limited transparency. The absence of robust internal controls and risk management systems makes both banks and businesses more vulnerable to internal fraud and external threats. Furthermore, the growing digitization of financial services, without corresponding investments in cybersecurity and digital literacy, has created new vulnerabilities—exposing supply chain participants to phishing attacks, data breaches, and identity fraud. Compounding the issue is the limited availability of advanced digital banking tools, such as real-time payment tracking, fraud detection algorithms, and automated reconciliation systems, which are crucial for operational efficiency and security. Addressing operational risk in Nepal will require a holistic investment in technology, training, governance, and regulatory oversight to ensure safer, more resilient financial operations across supply chains.

4. **Regulatory and Compliance Risk** Regulatory and compliance risk arises when financial institutions and supply chain participants struggle to adapt to complex and evolving legal frameworks. In Nepal, banks and businesses operate under the strict oversight of the Nepal Rastra Bank (NRB), which frequently updates regulations related to capital adequacy, foreign exchange controls, lending limits, and anti-money laundering (AML) requirements. While these measures are essential for maintaining financial stability and transparency, they can also pose

significant administrative and financial burdens, especially for small and medium-sized enterprises (SMEs) that may lack the expertise or resources to navigate compliance effectively. Additionally, the landscape is further complicated by frequent changes in tax laws, import-export regulations, and trade restrictions, which can disrupt operational planning and increase costs. Failure to comply with these regulations can result in penalties, delays in financial processing, or restrictions on international trade, thereby affecting supply chain continuity. To mitigate this risk, it is essential for businesses to invest in regulatory knowledge, digital compliance tools, and proactive engagement with policymakers. Strengthening institutional capacity and promoting clearer, more consistent regulatory guidelines will be key to reducing compliance-related disruptions in Nepal's supply chain ecosystem.

Strategies for Mitigating Financial Risks

1. Enhancing Credit Risk Management To mitigate credit risk, especially in contexts like Nepal where financial data is limited, businesses and financial institutions must adopt more robust credit evaluation frameworks. This includes integrating both traditional credit scoring models and alternative data sources—such as transaction history, utility payments, and supply chain performance—to assess creditworthiness. Establishing a centralized credit information bureau with up-to-date, accessible data can support more accurate risk profiling across industries. Businesses should also implement credit limits, payment terms, and collateral policies tailored to each customer's risk level. Encouraging the use of credit insurance, particularly for high-value transactions or international trade, can further protect against defaults. Additionally, fostering stronger relationships and regular communication with key buyers and suppliers helps in early detection of potential credit issues, enabling proactive decision-making. Digital tools and financial analytics platforms can enhance monitoring, allowing companies to track receivables in real time and respond quickly to irregularities. By taking a comprehensive and data-driven approach, organizations can significantly reduce exposure to credit-related losses.

- Implementing advanced credit scoring models
- Conducting thorough due diligence and risk assessments
- Encouraging the use of collateralized loans and trade credit insurance

2. Strengthening Liquidity Management Effective liquidity management is essential for ensuring the uninterrupted flow of goods and services in supply chains. In Nepal, where access to timely financing is often constrained, businesses can mitigate liquidity risk by adopting a proactive and diversified approach to cash flow planning. This includes maintaining realistic cash flow forecasts, monitoring working capital cycles closely, and identifying peak periods of financial strain in advance. Companies should establish multiple financing channels, such as short-term credit lines, supplier financing, invoice discounting, and factoring services to avoid overdependence on a single source of funds. Partnering with banks and fintech platforms that offer digital lending solutions and real-time payment processing can further enhance liquidity access, especially for SMEs. Internally, businesses should implement strong receivables and payables management practices, such as offering discounts for early payments, negotiating favorable terms with suppliers, and automating collections. By building cash reserves and improving transparency in financial reporting, companies can enhance their credibility with lenders and investors, positioning themselves to withstand temporary disruptions. Ultimately, strong liquidity management enables greater resilience and operational continuity in uncertain economic environments.

- Promoting supply chain financing solutions such as invoice discounting and factoring
- Encouraging digital payment solutions for faster transaction processing
- Diversifying banking relationships to reduce dependency on a single financial institution

3. Improving Operational Resilience Enhancing operational resilience is crucial for minimizing disruptions caused by internal inefficiencies, fraud, cyber threats, or technological failures. In Nepal's evolving financial and supply chain landscape, businesses should invest in strengthening internal controls, standardizing processes, and embracing digital transformation. This includes adopting enterprise resource planning (ERP) systems, automating repetitive tasks, and implementing real-time monitoring tools to detect anomalies early. Regular risk assessments, audits, and scenario planning help identify vulnerabilities in operations and build contingency plans. Cybersecurity must be prioritized through the deployment of firewalls, encryption protocols, two-factor authentication, and regular staff training to protect against increasing digital threats. Establishing a business continuity plan (BCP) and disaster recovery mechanisms ensures that operations can quickly recover from unexpected shocks such as system failures or supply chain disruptions. Collaboration with IT service providers and regulatory bodies can further enhance preparedness. By fostering a culture of resilience, adaptability, and compliance, organizations can maintain trust, avoid costly downtimes, and safeguard long-term stability.

- Investing in digital banking infrastructure and cybersecurity measures
- Enhancing risk management frameworks within banks and supply chain entities
- Conducting regular audits and compliance checks

4. Navigating Regulatory Challenges Effectively managing regulatory and compliance risks requires organizations to stay abreast of evolving laws, financial regulations, and trade policies—especially in countries like Nepal, where regulatory frameworks can change frequently. Businesses must establish dedicated compliance teams or officers responsible for monitoring updates from bodies such as the Nepal Rastra Bank (NRB), tax authorities, and trade regulators. Investing in compliance management software can streamline the process of tracking regulatory changes, managing documentation, and ensuring timely reporting. Additionally, fostering regular dialogue with regulatory institutions and industry associations helps businesses stay informed and voice concerns that may affect operations. For SMEs with limited capacity, leveraging outsourced legal and compliance advisory services can provide access to expert guidance at manageable costs. It's also important to provide internal training for employees on compliance practices to minimize the risk of inadvertent violations. By adopting a proactive, informed, and technology-enabled approach, companies can reduce the burden of compliance, avoid penalties, and ensure smoother integration into domestic and international markets.

- Engaging with regulatory bodies for policy advocacy and compliance assistance
- Training financial and supply chain professionals on evolving regulations
- Implementing robust reporting and documentation practices

Risk Management Framework and Policies

- **Develop a Comprehensive Risk Management Strategy:** Developing a comprehensive risk management strategy is essential for banks to effectively identify, assess, and mitigate various types of financial risks. A robust framework should address key risks such as credit risk, market risk, operational risk, and liquidity risk, ensuring that the bank can withstand potential disruptions. This involves creating well-defined risk policies and procedures that provide clear guidelines on how to manage each type of risk. The strategy should be dynamic, with regular reviews and updates to adapt to evolving market conditions, regulatory changes, and emerging risks. Additionally, the framework should include risk identification processes, assessment tools, and reporting mechanisms, ensuring that all levels of the organization are aligned in managing risk. By establishing such a strategy, banks can safeguard their financial health and maintain stability in times of uncertainty.

- **Implementing Enterprise Risk Management (ERM):** Implementing Enterprise Risk Management (ERM) is a critical step for banks to ensure a holistic approach to risk management across all areas of their operations. ERM models allow banks to identify, assess, and monitor risks not only in isolated departments but throughout the entire organization. By integrating risk management at every level—from front-line operations to senior management—banks can ensure that risks are understood and mitigated in a coordinated manner. This approach enables more timely and effective responses to both internal and external threats, whether they stem from financial markets, regulatory changes, cyberattacks, or operational failures. Moreover, ERM fosters a culture of risk awareness and accountability throughout the organization, ensuring that risk is a shared responsibility. By embedding risk management into the fabric of the organization, banks can better anticipate potential risks, minimize exposure, and make more informed strategic decisions, leading to greater resilience in the face of uncertainty.

Adoption of Advanced Technology

- **Digital Banking and Automation:** Digital banking and automation play a pivotal role in modernizing banks and reducing financial risks. By adopting digital banking services, banks can automate routine tasks, such as transaction processing, account management, and data entry, which significantly reduces the likelihood of human error and increases operational efficiency. Automation also helps banks handle larger volumes of transactions without compromising accuracy, ensuring smoother operations and faster response times. Furthermore, digital banking extends access to financial services beyond traditional brick-and-mortar branches, reaching underserved populations, particularly in rural or remote areas. This inclusion is crucial for improving financial access and stability, allowing more individuals and businesses to participate in the formal economy. Additionally, the use of digital platforms enhances customer convenience, leading to increased satisfaction and engagement, while allowing banks to offer a wider range of products and services at a lower cost. In sum, digital banking and automation not only mitigate operational risks but also drive greater financial inclusion, empowering both banks and their customers.

- **Cybersecurity Measures:** As digital banking and online financial services become more prevalent, the need for strong cybersecurity measures has never been more critical. With the rising frequency and sophistication of cyber threats, including hacking, phishing, and fraud, banks must implement robust cybersecurity frameworks to safeguard sensitive customer information and protect financial assets. These frameworks should include a combination of advanced encryption techniques, multi-factor authentication, firewalls, and intrusion detection systems to prevent unauthorized access and data breaches. Additionally, banks must regularly update and patch their systems to address vulnerabilities and stay ahead of emerging cyber risks. Employee training on cybersecurity best practices is also essential, as human error is often a key factor in security breaches. Furthermore, banks should establish clear protocols for incident response and disaster recovery, ensuring they can quickly mitigate the impact of any cyberattacks. By prioritizing cybersecurity, banks can build trust with customers, protect their reputations, and ensure the integrity of their digital platforms in an increasingly interconnected world.

- **Data Analytics:** Data analytics and artificial intelligence (AI) are becoming essential tools for banks in Nepal to enhance their risk management and decision-making processes. By leveraging advanced data analytics, banks can gain deep insights into customer behavior, market trends, and operational inefficiencies, enabling them to proactively identify emerging risks and opportunities. Predictive modeling, for instance, allows banks to assess the likelihood of credit defaults by analyzing historical data, helping them make more informed lending decisions. Additionally, AI algorithms can detect patterns in transactions that may indicate fraudulent activity, allowing banks to act swiftly and prevent losses. In terms of market risks, data analytics can help banks monitor economic indicators, exchange rate fluctuations, and other variables to forecast potential market shifts, allowing them to adjust their strategies accordingly. By incorporating data-driven approaches, banks in Nepal can improve the accuracy of their risk assessments, enhance operational efficiency, and offer more personalized services to customers, all while mitigating the financial risks associated with unforeseen events.

Enhancing Governance and Compliance

- **Strengthen Corporate Governance:** Strengthening corporate governance is crucial for banks to ensure that risk management processes are effectively followed and that the organization operates with transparency and accountability. Clear governance structures and well-defined roles and responsibilities for risk management are vital in aligning the bank's objectives with risk mitigation strategies. This includes assigning specific tasks to individuals or committees responsible for identifying, assessing, and managing various types of risks across the organization. By creating strong oversight mechanisms, such as independent audit committees and risk management boards, banks can ensure that risk management practices are not only in place but are regularly monitored and reviewed.

  Transparency in operations and decision-making is another key aspect of effective corporate governance. Banks should establish clear reporting lines and communication channels to ensure that stakeholders, including regulators, investors, and customers, are informed of the bank's risk exposure and mitigation strategies. Regular reporting on risk assessments, financial performance, and governance practices fosters trust and ensures that potential risks are identified early and addressed in a timely manner. Furthermore, a robust governance framework helps in maintaining ethical standards, reducing conflicts of interest, and promoting accountability at all levels of the bank, which ultimately contributes to the bank's long-term stability and growth.

- **Compliance with Regulatory Requirements:** Compliance with regulatory requirements is fundamental for ensuring the stability and legality of banking operations in Nepal. Adhering to the guidelines set by the Nepal Rastra Bank (NRB) and other relevant authorities helps banks avoid regulatory penalties and ensures they operate within the legal framework designed to protect the financial system. Regular audits, risk assessments, and compliance checks play a vital role in maintaining this adherence. Audits help identify any discrepancies or weaknesses in the bank's processes, while risk assessments ensure that potential threats are anticipated and mitigated in line with regulatory standards. Compliance checks, on the other hand, ensure that all departments are consistently following the established rules and regulations, minimizing the risk of non-compliance.

  By maintaining strict compliance, banks not only safeguard themselves against fines and operational disruptions but also build trust with customers, regulators, and investors. Furthermore, adherence to regulatory requirements supports the broader financial system's stability by ensuring that banks maintain sound financial practices, proper capital reserves, and effective risk management frameworks. In an environment where financial crimes, fraud, and global financial instability are prevalent, compliance helps banks maintain their reputation and protect their long-term viability in the market.

- **Anti-money Laundering (AML) and Know Your Customer (KYC):** Strict implementation of Anti-Money Laundering (AML) and Know Your Customer (KYC) norms is essential for mitigating the risk of financial crimes, including money laundering, fraud, and terrorist financing. These regulatory frameworks are designed to ensure that banks and financial institutions can identify, monitor, and report suspicious activities that may be associated with illegal or illicit transactions. By enforcing KYC procedures, banks are required to verify the identity of their customers, understand the nature of their business, and assess the risk associated with them. This helps prevent criminals from using the banking system to launder illicit funds or engage in fraudulent activities.

  AML measures go hand-in-hand with KYC by setting out the processes and systems to detect and prevent money laundering. Banks must monitor transactions for unusual patterns or large sums of money being transferred across borders, especially when customers have not provided adequate information or have complex, opaque business structures. With modern technologies like AI and machine learning, banks can enhance their AML and KYC processes, enabling them to detect suspicious activities more efficiently and accurately.

The strict enforcement of AML and KYC norms not only helps banks avoid legal and regulatory penalties but also ensures the integrity of the financial system. It also strengthens public trust, as customers and regulators can be confident that the bank is actively working to prevent financial crime and ensure that their transactions are safe and legitimate.

Insurance and Hedging Strategies

- **Credit Insurance:** Credit insurance is a valuable tool for banks to reduce their exposure to loan defaults and mitigate financial risk. By encouraging or offering credit insurance policies to clients, banks can protect themselves from the potential losses that arise when borrowers are unable to repay their loans. These insurance policies typically cover the risk of borrower default due to unforeseen events such as death, disability, or economic hardship. When a borrower defaults on a loan, the credit insurance policy compensates the bank for a significant portion of the outstanding debt, helping to minimize the financial impact.

  For banks, utilizing credit insurance helps maintain their capital reserves and ensures that their lending portfolio remains stable even in times of economic stress. It also allows banks to be more flexible in their lending practices, as they can mitigate the risk associated with higher-risk loans. On the client side, offering credit insurance helps borrowers feel more secure, knowing that their loan obligations are protected in case of unexpected circumstances.

  Moreover, credit insurance can serve as an additional risk management tool in sectors with high default rates or in regions experiencing economic volatility, providing a buffer against credit risk and promoting a more resilient financial system. Encouraging or integrating credit insurance into lending products ultimately helps safeguard both the bank's and the borrower's financial stability.

- **Hedging Against Commodity Price Volatility:** Hedging against commodity price volatility is a crucial strategy for banks in Nepal, especially considering the country's heavy dependence on agriculture. Agricultural commodities, such as rice, wheat, maize, and tea, are highly susceptible to price fluctuations driven by factors like weather conditions, global supply and demand, and geopolitical events. These price swings can have a significant impact on farmers, exporters, and the broader economy, affecting both revenues and financial stability.

  To mitigate the risks associated with commodity price volatility, banks can implement hedging strategies, such as using financial instruments like futures contracts, options, and swaps. These instruments allow banks and their clients to lock in future prices for commodities, providing protection against unfavorable price changes. For example, a bank could offer farmers or exporters the ability to hedge against a decline in the price of agricultural products, ensuring that they can secure a stable income regardless of market conditions.

  Additionally, banks can offer advisory services to clients, educating them on the benefits of hedging and how to use these tools effectively. By offering these financial products and services, banks help their clients manage risk and improve their financial resilience. Moreover, hedging strategies can help stabilize cash flows, which is particularly important for agriculture-based economies like Nepal, where seasonal variations and market unpredictability can otherwise cause significant financial disruptions.

  In the broader context, hedging can enhance the overall stability of the banking sector by reducing the potential for widespread loan defaults and economic instability due to commodity price shocks. This proactive risk management approach is key to protecting both the financial health of banks and the economic well-being of their agricultural clients.

Building Financial Resilience through Financial Inclusion

Promote Financial Inclusion: Promoting financial inclusion is a critical strategy for mitigating financial risk, particularly in countries like Nepal, where large portions of the population, especially in rural or remote areas, are underserved by traditional banking services. By expanding access to formal banking services, banks can diversify income sources and reduce the impact of local economic shocks. When more individuals and businesses have access to savings accounts, loans, insurance, and other financial products, they are better equipped to manage their finances, plan for the future, and withstand economic challenges, such as crop failures, natural disasters, or economic downturns.

Financial inclusion helps to stabilize the banking sector by broadening its customer base. A more diverse and inclusive client portfolio means that banks are less reliant on specific sectors or geographic regions, which can help mitigate risks from localized economic shocks. Additionally, by offering financial products tailored to the needs of underserved populations—such as microloans for small businesses or low-cost savings accounts—banks can help foster local economic growth and reduce financial instability in vulnerable areas.

Furthermore, as more people gain access to formal financial services, they are more likely to engage in the broader economy, leading to increased savings, investment, and consumption. This, in turn, can drive economic growth, which benefits the banking sector by creating a more resilient and vibrant financial ecosystem.

In the long term, promoting financial inclusion enhances the overall stability of the banking system, as a broader, more diverse customer base reduces the risks associated with relying on a narrow demographic. This strategy not only benefits individual customers but also strengthens the economy and the banking sector's ability to withstand shocks.

Microfinance and Cooperative Models: Supporting the growth of microfinance institutions (MFIs) and cooperative banking models is an effective way for banks in Nepal to spread financial risk across smaller, localized systems, thereby contributing to broader financial stability. Microfinance institutions provide small-scale loans to individuals or businesses that may not have access to traditional banking services, especially in rural or underserved areas. By focusing on microloans, MFIs help empower low-income individuals, particularly women, farmers, and small entrepreneurs, fostering economic inclusion and local development.

Cooperative banking models, on the other hand, are community-based financial institutions that are owned and managed by their members. These institutions often focus on serving local populations and have a unique advantage in understanding the specific needs and challenges of their communities. Cooperative banks can offer more personalized financial services, such as savings accounts, loans, and insurance products, which are tailored to the financial realities of their members.

Both microfinance and cooperative models play an important role in diversifying the financial system and reducing systemic risks. By decentralizing financial services, they spread risk across smaller, localized units, making the banking sector as a whole more resilient to regional economic shocks. For example, if one area faces economic hardship due to crop failure or natural disasters, the risk is mitigated because other regions with diverse economic activities are not affected in the same way. This helps stabilize both the banking sector and the local economies.

Moreover, these models often have a strong focus on social impact, supporting financial literacy, community development, and entrepreneurial growth. As these institutions grow, they contribute to greater financial stability by increasing access to credit, fostering savings, and providing risk management tools at the grassroots level. Supporting microfinance and cooperatives enhances financial inclusion, reduces poverty, and strengthens the overall resilience of the financial system, benefiting both individual customers and the broader economy.

Conclusion

Mitigating financial risk in Nepalese banking for supply chain management requires a multifaceted approach involving risk assessment, regulatory compliance, digital transformation, and financial innovation. By adopting proactive risk management strategies, banks and supply chain stakeholders can foster a more resilient and efficient financial ecosystem, ensuring sustained economic growth and stability in Nepal.

CHAPTER FOUR

Effective Inventory Management Strategies for MSMEs in Bihar India

Author: Ragini Singh, Research Scholar at Jai Prakash University Chhapra, Bihar

Abstract:

Effective inventory management is a critical challenge for Micro, Small, and Medium Enterprises (MSMEs) in Bihar, India, where resource constraints, limited access to technology, and fluctuating market conditions often hinder operational efficiency. This chapter explores the unique inventory management challenges faced by MSMEs in the region and presents practical strategies for improving inventory control and optimizing supply chain processes. It highlights the importance of adopting demand forecasting, just-in-time inventory systems, and technology-driven solutions such as inventory management software to enhance operational efficiency and reduce costs. Through a detailed analysis of local case studies, the chapter illustrates how MSMEs in Bihar can adopt cost-effective and scalable inventory management practices tailored to their specific needs. The chapter also discusses the role of training, government support, and collaboration with suppliers and distributors in fostering better inventory practices. Furthermore, it examines the impact of digital transformation on inventory management in small-scale enterprises and provides actionable recommendations for MSMEs to overcome logistical and financial barriers. Ultimately, this chapter emphasizes the need for a strategic approach to inventory management that enhances productivity, reduces waste, and ensures the sustainability of MSMEs in Bihar's evolving economic landscape.

Introduction

Micro, Small, and Medium Enterprises (MSMEs) are the backbone of Bihar's economy, playing a pivotal role in driving employment, fostering entrepreneurship, and contributing to the state's overall economic development. Despite their significance, many MSMEs in Bihar face persistent challenges in operational efficiency—one of the most critical being ineffective inventory management. Poor inventory practices often result in overstocking, stockouts, wastage, cash flow issues, and missed business opportunities, thereby impeding growth and sustainability. With limited access to capital and technology, many of these enterprises struggle to implement structured inventory systems, relying instead on manual or ad-hoc methods. This chapter delves into practical, scalable inventory management strategies that are tailored to the unique constraints and potential of Bihar's MSMEs. It highlights tools, techniques, and policy recommendations that can help these enterprises optimize stock levels, streamline operations, reduce costs, and improve profitability, ultimately strengthening their role in Bihar's economic ecosystem.

Key Inventory Management Challenges

1. **Limited Access to Technology** – A significant barrier to efficient inventory management among MSMEs in Bihar is the limited access to modern technology. Many enterprises continue to rely on manual tracking systems, such as paper-based records or basic spreadsheets, which are prone to human error, data duplication, and lack of real-time visibility. This outdated approach leads to frequent stock discrepancies, delayed reordering, and poor demand forecasting, ultimately affecting customer satisfaction and profitability. The high upfront costs of inventory management software, lack of digital literacy, and minimal technical support further discourage MSMEs from adopting advanced solutions. Additionally, limited internet connectivity and inadequate infrastructure in semi-urban and rural areas of Bihar compound the problem. Bridging this digital gap requires targeted interventions such as subsidized software tools, digital training programs, and support for cloud-based inventory systems, which can help MSMEs transition to more automated, accurate, and scalable inventory practices.

2. **Capital Constraints** – One of the most pressing issues faced by MSMEs in Bihar is limited access to working capital, which directly impacts their

ability to maintain optimal inventory levels. Due to cash flow challenges, many enterprises struggle to purchase raw materials or finished goods in bulk, often leading to understocking and missed sales opportunities. On the other hand, in an attempt to avoid stockouts, some MSMEs overstock, tying up valuable capital in unsold inventory that could have been better used for other operational needs. This delicate balancing act becomes even more difficult in the absence of reliable demand forecasts and flexible financing options. Furthermore, many MSMEs lack access to formal credit due to insufficient collateral, lack of financial documentation, and risk-averse lending practices by financial institutions. Addressing capital constraints requires innovative financing solutions such as inventory-based lending, invoice financing, government-backed credit schemes, and partnerships with microfinance institutions. By improving access to capital, MSMEs can make more strategic inventory decisions, improve turnover rates, and ultimately boost their profitability.

3. **Storage and Infrastructure Issues** – Inadequate warehousing and poor logistical infrastructure present significant obstacles to effective inventory management for MSMEs in Bihar. Many small enterprises operate in cramped or makeshift storage facilities that lack essential features such as proper shelving, climate control, security systems, and inventory tracking mechanisms. As a result, goods are often damaged, misplaced, or degraded, especially in the case of perishable items or sensitive raw materials. Additionally, poor transport connectivity and unreliable delivery networks—particularly in rural and semi-urban areas—cause delays in replenishment and distribution, making it difficult to align inventory levels with market demand. These challenges not only lead to increased operational costs but also contribute to stockouts, overstocking, and customer dissatisfaction. To overcome these issues, MSMEs need support in accessing affordable, shared warehousing solutions, improved logistics services, and public-private infrastructure development initiatives. Incorporating basic inventory layout planning and low-cost inventory tracking tools can also enhance stock control even within limited physical spaces.

4. **Supply Chain Disruptions** – MSMEs in Bihar frequently face supply chain disruptions that significantly hinder their ability to maintain consistent inventory levels. These disruptions often stem from seasonal demand fluctuations, where sudden spikes or drops in sales lead to

overstocking or stockouts. In addition, raw material shortages—caused by price volatility, delayed imports, or regional supply constraints—can halt production and strain business continuity. Transportation challenges, including poor road infrastructure, fuel price hikes, and logistical inefficiencies, further compound the problem by delaying inbound and outbound shipments. For MSMEs operating with limited buffer stock and minimal storage, such disruptions can have immediate financial repercussions, affecting customer satisfaction and business reputation. The impact is more severe in rural areas where supply chains are less resilient and alternatives are limited. To mitigate these risks, MSMEs must adopt flexible procurement strategies, build relationships with multiple suppliers, invest in basic demand forecasting tools, and explore local sourcing options to reduce dependency on external factors.

5. **Regulatory Compliance** – For MSMEs in Bihar, navigating the complexities of regulatory compliance adds an additional layer of difficulty to effective inventory management. Adhering to frameworks such as Goods and Services Tax (GST), local taxation laws, and state-level business regulations requires meticulous record-keeping and regular reporting. Inventory records must be accurate and up to date to comply with GST input and output calculations, which can be particularly burdensome for enterprises using manual or informal inventory tracking methods. Small businesses may also face challenges in classifying goods correctly, reconciling returns, or managing stock transfers between locations under different tax jurisdictions. Non-compliance, even if unintentional, can lead to penalties, delays in tax credits, and disruptions in cash flow. Moreover, the lack of dedicated compliance staff or access to professional advice puts additional pressure on MSME owners who already juggle multiple responsibilities. To ease this burden, there is a need for capacity-building programs, simplified compliance tools, digital inventory software with built-in tax modules, and greater support from local authorities to help MSMEs remain compliant without compromising operational efficiency.

Effective Inventory Management Strategies

1. Adopting Digital Inventory Tracking Embracing digital inventory tracking systems is a game-changing strategy for MSMEs seeking to improve efficiency, accuracy, and control over stock management. By shifting from manual record-keeping to computerized or cloud-based platforms, businesses can gain real-time visibility into stock levels, monitor product movement, and forecast demand more accurately. Affordable tools such as mobile-based apps, barcode scanning systems, and inventory management software like Zoho Inventory, Vyapar, or TallyPrime are increasingly accessible and user-friendly, even for small enterprises. These tools not only reduce human errors but also automate reordering, generate reports, track expiries, and support GST-compliant invoicing, which is crucial for regulatory adherence. Digital inventory tracking also facilitates better coordination with suppliers and distributors, enabling quicker response to market changes and disruptions. For MSMEs in Bihar, where operational efficiency is often hindered by resource constraints, adopting digital solutions—possibly with support from government or non-profit digital literacy initiatives—can significantly enhance competitiveness, reduce wastage, and improve profitability.

- Implementing affordable software like Tally, Zoho Inventory, or customized ERP solutions.
- Using barcoding and QR codes for efficient tracking.

2. Optimizing Stock Levels Maintaining the right balance between excess inventory and stockouts is critical for MSMEs, especially those operating with limited capital and storage capacity. Optimizing stock levels involves aligning inventory quantities with actual market demand to reduce holding costs, avoid wastage, and improve cash flow. Techniques such as Economic Order Quantity (EOQ) and ABC analysis can help MSMEs determine optimal reorder points and prioritize high-value items. Implementing Just-In-Time (JIT) inventory systems, where feasible, allows businesses to minimize stock on hand while ensuring timely replenishment. Regular demand forecasting, based on historical sales data and seasonal trends, also plays a vital role in inventory planning. For Bihar-based MSMEs, where supply chain unpredictability is common, it is important to maintain a small buffer or safety stock for critical items while avoiding overstocking low-demand goods. Digital tools can assist in tracking consumption patterns and generating automated alerts for reorder levels. By strategically managing inventory quantities, MSMEs can improve operational efficiency, reduce capital lock-in, and respond more swiftly to market fluctuations.

- Implementing Just-in-Time (JIT) inventory management to minimize holding costs.
- Categorizing inventory using ABC analysis to prioritize high-value items.

3. Improving Supply Chain Coordination Effective inventory management for MSMEs hinges on strong coordination across the supply chain, including suppliers, transporters, and distributors. Poor communication or lack of synchronization among stakeholders can lead to delays, stock mismatches, and missed opportunities. By building closer relationships and maintaining regular dialogue with suppliers, MSMEs can secure faster replenishment, flexible ordering terms, and better visibility into lead times and availability. Utilizing simple digital tools like WhatsApp groups, shared spreadsheets, or supply chain management apps can enhance real-time communication and reduce response time to changes in demand or disruptions. Establishing clear procurement schedules, sharing sales forecasts, and providing timely feedback can further streamline operations and improve planning accuracy. For MSMEs in Bihar, especially those operating in fragmented markets or rural areas, local supplier networks and cooperatives can be leveraged to reduce dependency on distant vendors and lower logistical risks. Ultimately, better supply chain coordination enables MSMEs to maintain lean inventories, cut down operational inefficiencies, and enhance service reliability.

- Establishing strong relationships with reliable suppliers to ensure timely procurement.
- Using demand forecasting to plan inventory based on historical sales data and market trends.

4. Enhancing Storage and Warehousing Efficiency Efficient storage and warehousing are essential components of effective inventory management, especially for MSMEs operating in space-constrained or resource-limited environments. Poorly organized storage can lead to damaged goods, misplaced stock, increased handling time, and inaccurate inventory counts. MSMEs in Bihar can benefit significantly from implementing basic warehouse management principles such as clear labeling, FIFO (First-In, First-Out) systems, and structured shelving arrangements. Even simple improvements like segregating raw materials from finished goods, using vertical storage racks, and assigning stock zones can enhance accessibility and reduce errors. Additionally, periodic stock audits and cycle counting help maintain accurate inventory records and prevent overstocking or stockouts. For businesses with limited individual storage space, exploring shared warehousing facilities or cluster-based storage solutions through industrial parks or MSME hubs can provide cost-effective alternatives. Integrating basic inventory management software that tracks stock location and movement within the warehouse further boosts operational efficiency. By optimizing storage practices, MSMEs can improve inventory accuracy, reduce spoilage, and enhance overall productivity.

- Utilizing vertical storage solutions to maximize space efficiency.
- Implementing FIFO (First-In, First-Out) and LIFO (Last-In, First-Out) methods to reduce wastage.

5. Reducing Waste and Shrinkage Minimizing waste and inventory shrinkage is critical for MSMEs to protect their margins and sustain profitability. Waste can occur due to overstocking, poor storage conditions, expiration of goods, or inefficient handling, while shrinkage typically results from theft, errors, or mismanagement. To tackle these issues, MSMEs must adopt a proactive approach to stock monitoring and control. Implementing techniques such as First-In, First-Out (FIFO) for perishable goods, conducting regular physical stock audits, and setting clear accountability systems for inventory handling can significantly reduce avoidable losses. Investing in basic security measures—like lockable storage, CCTV systems (where feasible), or simple inventory checklists—can also deter pilferage and unauthorized access. Moreover, digital inventory tracking tools can log every transaction and movement, making it easier to identify discrepancies and hold staff accountable. Training employees on proper storage practices, waste reduction techniques, and responsible stock handling further enhances efficiency. By reducing shrinkage and waste, MSMEs in Bihar can improve resource utilization, safeguard working capital, and boost long-term sustainability.

- Conducting regular audits to prevent pilferage and stock discrepancies.
- Training staff on proper inventory handling to minimize damages.

6. Leveraging Financial Strategies Access to the right financial tools is crucial for MSMEs to maintain healthy inventory levels without straining their working capital. By leveraging targeted financial strategies, MSMEs can better manage cash flow, invest in inventory, and reduce dependence on informal credit. Options such as inventory financing, invoice discounting, trade credit, and working capital loans from banks or microfinance institutions provide liquidity to purchase stock during peak demand or replenish depleted inventory. Government-backed schemes like the Credit Guarantee Fund Trust for Micro and Small Enterprises (CGTMSE) and MUDRA loans can offer accessible financing with reduced collateral requirements. Additionally, forming relationships with supplier networks that offer flexible payment terms—such as partial upfront payments or extended credit periods—can ease financial burdens. Digital bookkeeping and GST-compliant invoicing also improve creditworthiness and make it easier for MSMEs to access formal finance. By strategically utilizing financial tools and planning inventory purchases around seasonal trends and cash inflows, MSMEs can maximize turnover, prevent overextension, and build financial resilience.

- Using invoice financing and trade credit to manage working capital effectively.
- Taking advantage of government schemes and subsidies for MSMEs in Bihar.

Case Studies of Successful MSMEs in Bihar

- **Handloom & Textile Enterprises:** For handloom and textile enterprises—particularly prevalent in Bihar—adopting digital inventory tracking has proven to be a transformative step toward improving operational efficiency. Traditionally reliant on manual registers and informal systems, many of these businesses struggled with stock mismatches, material wastage, and delayed deliveries. By transitioning to simple digital tools such as inventory management software or mobile apps, enterprises can now monitor yarn usage, fabric stock, order status, and finished goods in real time. This shift has significantly reduced wastage, enabled better planning of raw material procurement, and improved order fulfillment accuracy and speed. Digital tracking also supports customized production scheduling, ensuring that designs and quantities align with customer preferences, thereby minimizing excess production. As a result, these businesses are better equipped to handle bulk orders, meet deadlines, and enhance customer satisfaction, while also improving their documentation for access to credit and government support schemes.

- **Agriculture-Based MSMEs:** Agriculture-based MSMEs in Bihar, such as those involved in food processing, dairy, or agro-trading, face significant challenges related to perishability and storage limitations. By adopting Just-In-Time (JIT) inventory practices and investing in basic warehouse improvements, many of these enterprises have managed to minimize spoilage and boost profitability. JIT enables timely procurement and production based on actual demand, reducing the need for long-term storage of perishable goods. When paired with simple storage upgrades—such as cold storage units, improved ventilation, and moisture control—these measures help preserve product quality and extend shelf life. Additionally, structured inventory layouts and real-time tracking help identify high-turnover items and eliminate redundant stock. This has not only reduced waste but also optimized resource allocation, allowing MSMEs to scale operations without overextending working capital. The result is a more responsive, efficient system that supports higher profit margins, better compliance with safety standards, and stronger market credibility.

Conclusion

Efficient inventory management is vital for the sustainability and growth of MSMEs in Bihar. By adopting digital tools, optimizing stock levels, and enhancing supply chain efficiency, businesses can reduce costs, improve cash flow, and boost productivity. With government support and technological advancements, Bihar's MSMEs can strengthen their inventory practices for long-term success.

CHAPTER FIVE

Optimizing Talent in the Supply Chain Ecosystem

Author: Dr. Mona Sharma, Assistant Professor | **Co-Author:** Miss. Siksha Rawat, Research Scholar

Abstract:

In today's dynamic and competitive business environment, optimizing talent within the supply chain ecosystem is critical for organizations seeking to enhance efficiency, innovation, and resilience. This chapter explores the evolving role of human capital in supply chain management, emphasizing the need for skilled professionals capable of adapting to technological advancements, global disruptions, and changing market demands. It examines strategies for attracting, developing, and retaining top talent in key areas such as logistics, procurement, data analytics, and supply chain leadership. The chapter also highlights the importance of continuous training, cross-functional collaboration, and fostering a culture of agility and innovation to optimize talent within the supply chain. Additionally, it discusses how digital tools, artificial intelligence, and automation are reshaping the skillsets required in the industry, and how organizations can leverage these changes to empower their workforce. Drawing on case studies and industry examples, the chapter provides actionable insights into how companies can create a talent-driven supply chain that supports both short-term performance and long-term strategic goals. Ultimately, it underscores the critical link between talent optimization and overall supply chain success in a rapidly evolving global marketplace.

1. Introduction

The supply chain ecosystem is undergoing rapid transformation, shaped by globalization, digitalization, and evolving customer expectations. Amid these shifts, talent has emerged as a critical differentiator in building agile, resilient, and innovative supply chains. Organizations are increasingly recognizing that their competitive edge depends not just on systems and technology, but on the people who design, manage, and operate those systems. This chapter explores the strategic importance of talent in the supply chain, identifies emerging challenges and opportunities, and presents frameworks and best practices for optimizing talent throughout the ecosystem.

2. The Talent Gap in Supply Chain Management

Recent industry reports consistently highlight a growing talent gap in supply chain functions. According to Deloitte and MHI, nearly 60% of supply chain leaders report difficulty in finding qualified professionals. This gap is driven by the increasing complexity of supply chains, the integration of new technologies such as AI and robotics, and a generational shift in workforce preferences.

Traditional supply chain roles are evolving. Today's professionals must possess hybrid skills—combining operational expertise with digital fluency, analytical thinking, and cross-functional collaboration. Without targeted strategies to close the talent gap, organizations risk operational inefficiencies, reduced innovation, and limited adaptability.

3. Strategic Talent Acquisition

Optimizing talent begins with strategic acquisition, which requires moving beyond traditional, reactive hiring models toward a more proactive and forward-thinking approach. In the dynamic supply chain landscape, where skills in data analytics, logistics technology, and sustainability are increasingly in demand, organizations must focus on building a talent pipeline aligned with future needs. This includes engaging with academic institutions and vocational training centers to attract emerging talent, leveraging industry partnerships and internship programs, and utilizing data-driven recruitment tools to identify skill gaps and predict workforce trends. Additionally, developing a strong employer brand, offering flexible and purpose-driven roles, and embracing diversity and inclusion strategies are critical for attracting high-caliber candidates. By investing in workforce planning, talent mapping, and ongoing candidate engagement, companies can ensure they are not just filling positions, but acquiring individuals who align with their long-term strategic goals and evolving supply chain demands.This includes:

Competency-Based Hiring: To build a future-ready supply chain workforce, organizations must embrace competency-based hiring—a recruitment approach that prioritizes skills, behaviors, and knowledge over traditional credentials. Rather than focusing solely on academic qualifications or years of experience, this method emphasizes identifying candidates who demonstrate core competencies aligned with emerging supply chain trends and challenges. Key competencies for modern supply chains include systems thinking, which enables individuals to understand and manage complex, interconnected processes; data analytics, essential for interpreting supply chain metrics and making data-driven decisions; and sustainability literacy, which supports environmentally and socially responsible practices. By clearly defining these competencies and integrating them into job descriptions, interview questions, and assessment tools, organizations can more effectively identify candidates with the agility, problem-solving ability, and strategic mindset needed to thrive in a fast-evolving supply chain environment. Competency-based hiring not only ensures better talent alignment but also enhances long-term workforce adaptability and performance.

Employer Branding: In an increasingly competitive talent market, strong employer branding is essential to attract and retain top-tier candidates—especially from younger generations seeking meaningful and forward-looking careers. For the supply chain function, which is often viewed as a back-end or operational role, there is a growing need to reframe it as a dynamic, tech-enabled, and impactful field. Organizations must actively promote the supply chain as a hub of innovation, sustainability, and strategic decision-making, highlighting how it contributes to global connectivity, customer satisfaction, and environmental stewardship. Showcasing employee success stories, career growth opportunities, and digital transformation initiatives on platforms like LinkedIn, career sites, and campus recruitment events can position the organization as an employer of choice. Additionally, emphasizing values that resonate with Gen Z and millennials—such as diversity, flexibility, purpose, and ESG (Environmental, Social, and Governance) impact—can make the supply chain function more appealing. A compelling employer brand not only draws in high-potential candidates but also fosters greater engagement, loyalty, and pride among current employees.

Diversity and Inclusion: In today's interconnected and globalized supply chain environment, diversity and inclusion (D&I) are not just ethical imperatives—they are strategic advantages. Building diverse teams that bring together varied cultural backgrounds, gender identities, experiences, and problem-solving approaches leads to richer insights, greater creativity, and more resilient decision-making. Research consistently shows that diverse teams outperform homogeneous ones in terms of innovation, collaboration, and financial performance. In supply chains, where challenges are multifaceted and often cross geographic and functional boundaries, inclusive teams are better equipped to adapt, communicate effectively, and solve problems from multiple angles. To cultivate D&I, organizations must go beyond tokenism by embedding inclusive practices into recruitment, leadership development, team dynamics, and workplace culture. This includes removing unconscious bias from hiring, promoting equitable career progression, and creating safe spaces for all voices to be heard. By prioritizing diversity and fostering inclusion, companies not only reflect the global markets they serve but also build agile, innovative, and high-performing supply chain teams.

Partnerships with academic institutions, apprenticeships, and internships can also help bridge the gap between education and industry needs.

4. Talent Development and Retention

Attracting talent is only the first step—developing and retaining that talent is crucial for sustaining a high-performing supply chain workforce. Organizations must invest in continuous learning, career progression, and employee engagement to ensure long-term commitment and growth. This includes structured training programs, mentorship opportunities, leadership development tracks, and exposure to cross-functional projects that broaden skills and strategic thinking. With supply chains becoming increasingly data-driven and technology-enabled, reskilling employees in areas like AI, automation, analytics, and digital tools is vital to keep pace with evolving demands. Equally important is fostering a workplace culture that promotes purpose, recognition, work-life balance, and psychological safety, all of which contribute to job satisfaction and reduce turnover. Personalized development plans, regular feedback loops, and transparent internal mobility options help employees envision a future within the organization. By nurturing talent from within, companies not only safeguard institutional knowledge but also build resilient and adaptive teams that can confidently navigate supply chain complexity and change.

Once talent is onboarded, development becomes key to long-term optimization. This requires:

Continuous Learning: In the face of rapid technological advancement and shifting global dynamics, continuous learning has become a cornerstone of effective talent development in the supply chain ecosystem. Organizations must prioritize upskilling and reskilling initiatives that not only address current skill gaps but also anticipate future capabilities needed to drive competitiveness and innovation. Programs focused on emerging technologies—such as AI, robotics, blockchain, data analytics, and digital supply chain platforms—enable employees to stay ahead of the curve and contribute meaningfully to business transformation. Additionally, learning should be strategically aligned with organizational goals, ensuring that employees are developing competencies that directly impact operational efficiency, customer satisfaction, and sustainability targets. Offering flexible learning formats, including microlearning, online modules, certifications, and hands-on workshops, encourages participation across different roles and experience levels. By fostering a culture of lifelong learning, organizations empower their workforce to adapt to change, solve complex challenges, and continuously drive value throughout the supply chain.

Mentorship and Coaching: Mentorship and coaching play a vital role in nurturing talent and fostering long-term career growth within the supply chain workforce. By establishing both formal and informal support systems, organizations can create environments where employees receive guidance, feedback, and encouragement tailored to their individual goals and challenges. Formal mentorship programs connect less experienced staff with seasoned professionals, facilitating knowledge transfer in critical areas such as strategic sourcing, logistics, and supply chain analytics. Informal coaching relationships, including peer mentoring and on-the-job learning, help cultivate confidence, problem-solving skills, and cross-functional collaboration. These relationships not only accelerate skill development but also boost engagement, morale, and a sense of belonging. Coaching, in particular, supports high-potential employees and emerging leaders by providing structured, future-focused development aligned with business objectives. Ultimately, a strong mentorship and coaching culture contributes to higher retention rates, greater employee satisfaction, and a more agile, leadership-ready workforce equipped to thrive in evolving supply chain environments.

Engagement Strategies: Effective employee engagement is a key driver of retention, productivity, and performance, especially in fast-paced and high-pressure environments like supply chain management. To keep high performers motivated and committed, organizations must adopt comprehensive engagement strategies that reflect evolving workforce expectations. This begins with regular feedback mechanisms, such as pulse surveys, one-on-one check-ins, and open forums, which give employees a voice and foster a culture of transparency and trust. Flexible work models—including hybrid schedules, remote options, and results-based performance evaluation—promote work-life balance and autonomy, which are especially valued by today's diverse and multigenerational workforce. Additionally, recognition programs that celebrate both individual and team achievements help reinforce desired behaviors and boost morale. Whether through formal rewards, peer recognition platforms, or career advancement opportunities, acknowledging contributions in meaningful ways strengthens loyalty and encourages continued excellence. By creating a supportive and adaptive work environment, organizations can better retain top supply chain talent, reduce turnover, and build resilient teams capable of driving sustained growth and innovation.

Talent retention is not just about compensation but about creating purpose-driven work environments that align individual goals with organizational vision.

5. Technology and Talent Synergy

As supply chains rapidly evolve into digitally integrated ecosystems, the synergy between technology and talent becomes a critical enabler of performance and innovation. Emerging technologies such as the Internet of Things (IoT), blockchain, machine learning, and robotic process automation (RPA) are reshaping traditional workflows, redefining roles, and creating new opportunities for value creation. However, the goal is not to replace human talent—but to amplify it. These technologies excel at handling repetitive, data-intensive tasks, allowing human workers to focus on strategic thinking, creativity, and decision-making. For example, AI-powered analytics can provide insights, but it's skilled professionals who interpret the results and act on them. Likewise, IoT devices can track assets in real time, but it's human judgment that determines the operational response. To fully realize this synergy, organizations must invest in digital literacy, change management, and cross-training programs that help employees embrace technology as a collaborative partner. By aligning human potential with technological capability, companies can build smarter, more agile, and resilient supply chains that are equipped for future challenges.**Digital Literacy:** Employees must be equipped to interpret data, utilize supply chain software, and collaborate with AI systems.

Human-Centered Design: As digital tools become more embedded in supply chain operations, applying a human-centered design approach is essential to ensure that technology serves to empower rather than overwhelm the workforce. This design philosophy prioritizes the needs, capabilities, and experiences of the people who use the technology—whether they are warehouse operators, logistics planners, or procurement specialists. By involving end users early in the development or adoption process, organizations can ensure that new systems are intuitive, accessible, and aligned with actual workflows. For instance, dashboards should display data in user-friendly formats, automation interfaces should require minimal technical training, and mobile apps should accommodate workers in dynamic field environments. Human-centered technology fosters confidence, efficiency, and engagement, reducing resistance to change and improving adoption rates. Moreover, it reinforces the idea that digital transformation is a collaborative evolution rather than a top-down disruption. By designing technology around human strengths—like critical thinking, empathy, and adaptability—organizations can create a more inclusive, effective, and future-ready supply chain workforce.

A dual investment in people and technology fosters a more responsive and intelligent supply chain.

6. Collaboration Across the Ecosystem

In today's interconnected global economy, optimizing talent in the supply chain requires collaboration that extends beyond organizational boundaries. Building a robust supply chain talent ecosystem involves strategic partnerships with academia, government agencies, technology providers, industry associations, and even competitors. Collaborative efforts such as joint training programs, co-designed curricula, internships, and research initiatives with universities can help align education with the evolving needs of the supply chain sector. Similarly, public-private partnerships can bridge skill gaps through policy support, workforce development incentives, and infrastructure enhancements. Technology vendors and consulting firms can also play a crucial role by co-developing tools and upskilling programs tailored to real-world challenges. Additionally, cross-industry collaboration facilitates the exchange of best practices, innovation, and shared resources, especially in areas like sustainability, risk management, and digital transformation. By fostering a culture of open knowledge-sharing, mutual growth, and collective problem-solving, organizations can ensure a steady pipeline of agile, well-rounded talent ready to navigate the complexity of modern supply chains.

No single entity can optimize talent in isolation. Effective talent ecosystems require coordinated efforts among:

- **Academia:** Academic institutions are pivotal collaborators in building a future-ready supply chain workforce. By co-creating curricula that reflect current and emerging industry needs, universities and colleges can better prepare students for the dynamic realities of supply chain roles. This involves incorporating practical skills such as data analytics, digital tools, sustainability practices, risk management, and global logistics into traditional business and operations programs. Collaborative efforts—such as guest lectures from industry leaders, joint research initiatives, capstone projects, and real-world internships—help bridge the gap between theory and practice. Moreover, academic partnerships can serve as innovation hubs, where new models of supply chain thinking and problem-solving are tested and refined. Continuous dialogue between educators and supply chain professionals ensures that learning remains relevant, adaptive, and forward-looking. By aligning academic outputs with industry demands, these partnerships contribute to a steady talent pipeline equipped to lead and transform supply chains in an era of rapid change.
- **Industry Partners:** Industry partners play a crucial role in shaping and strengthening the supply chain talent landscape through active knowledge-sharing and co-development initiatives. By sharing best practices, case studies, and operational insights, companies can help create a collective learning environment that elevates the entire ecosystem. These collaborations often lead to the co-development of training platforms, simulation tools, and certification programs tailored to real-world challenges—ranging from procurement strategy and inventory optimization to digital transformation and sustainability. Industry players can also support on-the-job training, apprenticeships, and mentorship programs, offering learners hands-on experience and exposure to evolving technologies like AI, IoT, and blockchain. Through forums, roundtables, and joint task forces, industry partners help

identify skill gaps and anticipate future talent needs. This collective approach not only boosts organizational capabilities but also ensures that the broader supply chain community remains agile, innovative, and competitive in a rapidly changing global market.

- **Government and NGOs:** Governments and non-governmental organizations (NGOs) are essential enablers in fostering a skilled and resilient supply chain workforce. Through policy frameworks, funding initiatives, and regulatory support, these institutions can create an environment conducive to workforce development and inclusive economic growth. Governments can offer incentives for upskilling and reskilling programs, tax benefits for training investments, and support for vocational education centers focused on logistics, manufacturing, and technology. Public policy can also promote industry-academia collaboration, encourage the adoption of emerging technologies, and prioritize job creation in high-potential sectors. NGOs complement these efforts by delivering grassroots-level training, advocating for equitable access to opportunities, and addressing the needs of marginalized communities, especially in developing regions. Together, these actors can facilitate the development of national and regional talent strategies, create platforms for dialogue between stakeholders, and support innovation in learning methodologies. Their involvement ensures that talent development is not just a corporate initiative, but a collective movement toward building a sustainable and future-ready supply chain ecosystem.

These collaborations enhance talent mobility, drive innovation, and build more resilient supply chains.

7. Case Studies and Best Practices Real-world examples provide powerful insights into how leading organizations are effectively optimizing talent within the evolving supply chain landscape. These case studies and best practices illustrate how strategic talent initiatives—rooted in innovation, collaboration, and adaptability—translate into measurable performance gains. For instance, Zara has successfully built a responsive and agile workforce by tightly integrating design, production, and logistics teams, enabling quick reaction to fashion trends and consumer demand. Amazon demonstrates excellence in workforce automation and augmentation, blending robotics and AI with skilled human oversight to streamline fulfillment operations. In contrast, Procter & Gamble focuses on continuous learning and leadership development across its global supply network, empowering employees to drive localized solutions within a standardized framework. Meanwhile, Unilever's Future Fit initiative emphasizes upskilling and sustainability training as core components of its talent strategy. These examples highlight that there is no one-size-fits-all approach—but common themes include digital fluency, human-centered leadership, cross-functional collaboration, and lifelong learning. By analyzing and adopting these best practices, organizations can craft their own roadmaps for talent resilience and supply chain excellence.

Unilever has launched a global supply chain talent program focused on experiential learning and cross-border rotations, resulting in increased employee engagement and innovation.

Amazon invests heavily in training initiatives such as Career Choice, offering tuition support for supply chain-relevant education.

Maersk emphasizes leadership development through immersive simulations and global exposure, building succession-ready leaders in logistics.

These examples highlight that investment in talent directly correlates with performance, agility, and competitive advantage.

8. Future Outlook The future of supply chain talent lies at the intersection of technology, adaptability, and human-centered innovation. As global supply chains become increasingly complex, digitized, and sustainability-driven, the demand for a versatile, tech-savvy, and resilient workforce will intensify. Skills in areas such as data science, cybersecurity, AI integration, circular economy, and stakeholder collaboration will become essential, not optional. The workplace itself will continue evolving—with hybrid models, cross-border teams, and gig-based roles becoming more prevalent. Organizations that proactively invest in continuous learning, inclusive leadership, and agile workforce planning will be best positioned to thrive. Furthermore, the growing focus on ESG (Environmental, Social, and Governance) goals will drive companies to develop supply chain talent that can balance efficiency with ethical responsibility. In this changing landscape, success will not only depend on acquiring the right skills but on creating a culture that values curiosity, collaboration, and a growth mindset. The future belongs to those who view talent not just as a resource—but as a strategic differentiator in building adaptive, sustainable, and globally competitive supply chains.

As we approach 2030, several trends will shape the talent landscape:

AI-Augmented Roles: As artificial intelligence becomes more deeply embedded in supply chain operations, the nature of work is shifting from automation to augmentation. Rather than replacing human roles, AI is increasingly being used to enhance human decision-making, creativity, and efficiency. In this evolving landscape, humans and machines will co-create solutions, giving rise to what's known as collaborative intelligence—a synergy where machines handle data-heavy, repetitive tasks while humans focus on strategic thinking, problem-solving, and interpersonal coordination. For example, AI-powered demand forecasting tools can provide deep insights, but it's up to skilled supply chain professionals to interpret the results, adjust strategies, and navigate uncertainties. Similarly, warehouse robots may handle picking and packing, but human workers oversee system optimization and ensure smooth operations. This human-machine partnership demands a new skill set, blending technological literacy with emotional intelligence, adaptability, and systems thinking. Preparing talent for AI-augmented roles means investing not only in technical training but also in redefining job roles, fostering collaboration, and building trust in AI systems. It marks a fundamental shift—from working with technology to working alongside it, shaping a more intelligent, resilient, and responsive supply chain workforce.

Sustainable Skillsets: As global focus intensifies on ethical and environmentally responsible business practices, sustainability is no longer a niche concern—it is a core competency in modern supply chain management. Professionals in the field must now possess a working knowledge of ESG (Environmental, Social, and Governance) principles, as these directly influence sourcing decisions, logistics strategies, supplier relationships, and overall brand reputation. Future-ready supply chain roles will require skillsets that include carbon footprint analysis, ethical sourcing, circular economy models, regulatory compliance, and stakeholder engagement around sustainability goals. Moreover, understanding sustainability reporting standards and being able to measure and communicate environmental and social impact will be essential. Organizations are increasingly seeking talent that can align operational performance with broader ESG objectives, ensuring that supply chains are not only efficient but also transparent, responsible, and resilient. Cultivating these sustainable skillsets across all levels of the supply chain workforce—from procurement officers to logistics planners—will be key to achieving long-term value creation and global competitiveness.

Gig and Hybrid Work Models: The rise of gig and hybrid work models is reshaping how supply chain organizations attract, manage, and retain talent. Driven by digital connectivity, evolving worker expectations, and the need for greater agility, these flexible arrangements allow professionals to engage in project-based, remote, or part-time roles—opening up access to global talent pools while offering employees more autonomy and work-life balance. In the supply chain context, this shift means that traditional full-time, on-site roles are giving way to dynamic team structures, where contractors, freelancers, and remote specialists collaborate alongside core teams. However, with flexibility comes complexity. Organizations must embrace adaptive leadership approaches, capable of managing decentralized teams, fostering engagement across time zones, and ensuring consistent performance. Additionally, new retention strategies are needed—ones that prioritize personalized development opportunities, purpose-driven work, and meaningful connection over conventional perks. As the line between permanent and freelance work continues to blur, successful supply chain leaders will be those who can build inclusive, agile cultures that thrive in both physical and virtual environments.

Preparing for these trends involves foresight, adaptability, and a commitment to lifelong learning.

9. Conclusion

Talent optimization is not a one-time initiative but a continuous, strategic priority. As supply chains become more interconnected and digitized, organizations must invest in acquiring, developing, and retaining talent that can thrive amid complexity. By fostering collaboration across academia, industry, and government, and by aligning technology with human potential, the supply chain ecosystem can become a powerful engine of innovation and resilience.

CHAPTER SIX

Social impact of microfinance in circular economy

Author: Pushkar Kumar Singh, Research Scholar at Jai Prakash University Chhapra Bihar

Abstract:

Microfinance has long been celebrated as a tool for economic inclusion, providing financial services to individuals and communities who lack access to traditional banking systems. In the context of the circular economy, which emphasizes resource efficiency, waste reduction, and sustainability, microfinance plays a pivotal role in promoting inclusive economic growth while addressing environmental challenges.

This paper explores the intersection of microfinance and the circular economy, focusing on the social impact that microfinance initiatives can have in driving sustainable development. By enabling small-scale entrepreneurs and marginalized communities to access capital, microfinance supports business models that align with circular principles—such as recycling, product reuse, and resource efficiency. These businesses contribute to reducing waste, promoting sustainable production practices, and encouraging environmentally responsible consumption.

Additionally, microfinance programs in the circular economy foster social benefits, such as job creation, poverty reduction, and empowerment, particularly for women and underserved populations. The integration of financial services with circular economy initiatives helps to create sustainable livelihoods, improve community resilience, and promote social equity.

This paper also examines the challenges and opportunities that arise when aligning microfinance with circular economy goals, including the need for tailored financial products, capacity building, and collaboration between financial institutions, policymakers, and social enterprises. The findings suggest that the combination of microfinance and circular economy principles offers a transformative pathway for fostering both social and environmental sustainability in developing economies.

Ultimately, the social impact of microfinance within the circular economy is profound, creating a bridge between financial inclusion and environmental sustainability, and contributing to a more resilient, equitable, and sustainable future.

Introduction

Microfinance plays a crucial role in fostering economic development by providing financial access to underserved communities. In the context of the circular economy, microfinance enables small businesses and entrepreneurs to adopt sustainable practices, reduce waste, and create value from recycled or repurposed materials. This chapter explores the social impact of microfinance in promoting circular economy principles, particularly in marginalized and low-income communities.

Role of Microfinance in the Circular Economy

Microfinance institutions (MFIs) are emerging as critical enablers in the shift toward a circular economy, particularly in developing regions where access to traditional financing is limited. By offering small-scale, inclusive financial services, MFIs empower local entrepreneurs, artisans, and small businesses that embrace circular principles—such as reuse, recycling, remanufacturing, and sustainable production. These may include ventures focused on turning waste into raw materials, repairing and refurbishing products, or creating eco-friendly alternatives to traditional goods. MFIs help these enterprises overcome financial barriers by providing micro-loans, savings mechanisms, and business training, often tailored to low-income and marginalized communities. This support not only fosters local innovation but also promotes resource efficiency, job creation, and environmental stewardship. Furthermore, MFIs often work in partnership with NGOs, government bodies, and sustainability-focused investors to scale impact and integrate circular economy goals into community development strategies. As such, microfinance serves as both a financial catalyst and social accelerator in building resilient, regenerative economic systems. Microfinance enables:

1. **Access to Capital for Green Businesses** – One of the most significant contributions of microfinance to the circular economy is its role in bridging the capital gap for green entrepreneurs. Traditional banking institutions often view small-scale, sustainability-focused ventures as high-risk or unprofitable, especially in rural or underserved areas. Microfinance institutions (MFIs), however, provide accessible, low-barrier financing tailored to the needs of these emerging eco-businesses. This enables small entrepreneurs to launch or scale circular business models—such as organic farming, composting initiatives, upcycled product lines, and renewable energy services—without being constrained by the rigid criteria of formal banks. Through micro-loans and flexible repayment plans, MFIs empower local innovators to adopt sustainable practices, invest in eco-friendly equipment, and develop community-based solutions that support both environmental and economic well-being. In doing so, microfinance not only drives financial inclusion but also becomes a key engine for green economic transformation.

2. **Encouraging Resource Efficiency** – Microfinance plays a pivotal role in promoting resource efficiency among micro and small enterprises, particularly those striving to align with circular economy principles. By offering targeted financial assistance, MFIs enable businesses to invest in technologies, tools, and practices that minimize waste, extend product life cycles, and optimize the use of raw materials. This includes funding for equipment that supports recycling, energy-efficient production methods, water-saving irrigation systems, or material recovery processes. Such investments, though modest in size, can significantly enhance productivity and environmental performance, especially for businesses operating in resource-constrained settings. Moreover, MFIs often pair financial products with capacity-building programs that educate entrepreneurs on sustainable operations, helping them integrate eco-efficiency into their business models. This dual approach—capital plus knowledge—empowers enterprises to do more with less, creating long-term economic value while contributing to the preservation of natural resources. As a result, microfinance becomes not just a financial tool, but a driver of sustainable innovation at the grassroots level.

3. **Job Creation and Economic Inclusion** – Microfinance serves as a powerful vehicle for inclusive economic growth by funding circular economy ventures that generate employment—especially for women,

youth, and marginalized communities. Circular businesses, by their nature, often rely on labor-intensive processes such as repair, refurbishment, recycling, and artisanal upcycling, which are ideally suited for community-based, small-scale operations. When MFIs provide access to capital and entrepreneurial training, they help individuals who might otherwise be excluded from formal labor markets to create their own livelihoods. Women, in particular, benefit significantly, as many circular businesses—like sustainable textiles, eco-crafts, and organic food production—are closely aligned with sectors where women already have cultural and practical experience. These enterprises not only generate jobs but also foster community resilience, social empowerment, and environmental responsibility. In this way, microfinance contributes to both the economic democratization and the environmental sustainability goals of the circular economy, proving that small investments can lead to transformative social impact.

Social Benefits of Microfinance in the Circular Economy

1. Poverty Alleviation Microfinance plays a crucial role in breaking the cycle of poverty by providing low-income individuals with the financial means to start and grow small businesses—many of which align with circular economy principles. Through small loans, savings schemes, and financial literacy programs, microfinance empowers people who lack access to traditional banking services to become economically self-reliant. In circular enterprises—such as recycling, composting, repair services, and eco-friendly manufacturing—microfinance enables income generation while promoting sustainable practices. These businesses often require low capital investment but can deliver steady revenue and employment, particularly in underserved rural and urban communities. Moreover, by fostering local entrepreneurship, microfinance not only improves individual livelihoods but also stimulates community-level economic development, reducing dependency on external aid. The result is a dual benefit: economic upliftment for the poor and environmental stewardship, making microfinance a vital tool in achieving inclusive and sustainable development.

- Microfinance empowers low-income individuals to start sustainable businesses, enhancing their financial independence.

- It fosters economic resilience by reducing reliance on single-use resources and promoting regenerative practices.

2. Women's Empowerment Microfinance has been a transformative force in advancing women's empowerment, especially when aligned with circular economy initiatives. By offering women access to capital—often for the first time—MFIs enable them to start or expand eco-conscious businesses such as organic farming, textile recycling, biodegradable packaging production, or upcycled crafts. These ventures not only generate income but also promote environmental sustainability. Beyond financial independence, microfinance fosters social empowerment, as women gain decision-making authority within their households and communities. Many MFIs also provide capacity-building programs that enhance women's skills in entrepreneurship, leadership, and sustainable practices, further amplifying their confidence and community influence. In rural and underserved regions, this empowerment has a ripple effect, improving family well-being, children's education, and health outcomes. By integrating women into the green economy, microfinance supports gender-inclusive development while driving sustainable local innovation—making it a cornerstone for equitable and regenerative economic systems.

- Many MFIs focus on women-led enterprises, fostering gender equality and financial inclusion.
- Women entrepreneurs engaged in circular economy activities, such as textile recycling or organic farming, gain economic stability.

3. Community Development Microfinance acts as a catalyst for community development by financing small-scale circular businesses that generate both economic and environmental value within local areas. When individuals are empowered to start eco-friendly enterprises—such as waste recycling centers, composting hubs, or repair and resale shops—these initiatives not only create jobs but also address local challenges, such as pollution, resource scarcity, and unemployment. The reinvestment of earnings and skills into the community fosters a sense of ownership, resilience, and collaboration among residents. Many microfinance-supported projects also operate on cooperative or group lending models, which further strengthen social bonds and collective action. In this way, microfinance promotes inclusive growth that is not just individualistic, but community-oriented, enhancing infrastructure, improving environmental conditions, and uplifting entire neighborhoods. By rooting circular economy practices at the grassroots level, MFIs play a critical role in building sustainable, self-reliant communities capable of adapting to economic and ecological changes.

- Circular economy-based businesses contribute to cleaner environments by reducing pollution and waste.
- Sustainable enterprises strengthen local supply chains and create self-sufficient economies.

4. Environmental Sustainability Microfinance plays a vital role in advancing environmental sustainability by empowering small entrepreneurs to adopt circular business models that reduce waste, conserve natural resources, and lower carbon footprints. With access to targeted financial products, individuals and microenterprises can invest in eco-friendly technologies and sustainable practices, such as solar-powered equipment, organic farming inputs, water recycling systems, and biodegradable materials. These green investments, though often small in scale, collectively contribute to larger environmental goals like climate change mitigation, pollution reduction, and biodiversity conservation. Additionally, by promoting reuse, repair, and recycling, microfinance-funded ventures help shift communities away from a linear "take-make-dispose" economy toward a regenerative circular model. Many MFIs also integrate environmental education and training into their programs, raising awareness of sustainable practices among borrowers. In doing so, microfinance not only supports livelihood development but also cultivates a culture of environmental responsibility—ensuring that economic progress goes hand-in-hand with ecological preservation.

- Microfinance supports renewable energy projects, waste management initiatives, and eco-friendly production methods.
- It promotes ethical consumerism and responsible production.

Challenges and Future Prospects

While microfinance has demonstrated significant potential in fostering circular economy practices, several challenges still hinder its full impact. One of the primary barriers is the limited financial literacy among borrowers, which can lead to poor loan utilization and repayment difficulties. Many microenterprises also face market access constraints, lacking the infrastructure or networks needed to scale their sustainable products and services. Additionally, MFIs themselves may struggle with resource limitations, technological gaps, and difficulties in assessing the viability of circular business models. Environmental risk assessments and impact measurement frameworks are often underdeveloped. Despite these hurdles, the future holds promising prospects. Advancements in digital finance, mobile banking, and blockchain technology offer new ways to expand reach, reduce costs, and improve transparency. As global attention intensifies on climate action and inclusive growth, there is increasing scope for public-private partnerships, green microfinance products, and supportive policy frameworks to bolster the sector. With strategic innovation and collaboration, microfinance can evolve into a powerful enabler of a just, inclusive, and sustainable circular economy.

Despite its benefits, microfinance in the circular economy faces challenges such as limited awareness, regulatory barriers, and difficulty in assessing loan viability for sustainable businesses. Future strategies include:

- **Enhancing Financial Literacy** – Improving financial literacy is essential for ensuring that microfinance truly empowers borrowers to engage in sustainable and successful circular economy ventures. Many micro-entrepreneurs lack the knowledge required to manage finances effectively, assess business risks, or understand the long-term benefits of environmentally sustainable practices. By incorporating education on circular economy principles, MFIs can help clients not only understand the basics of saving, budgeting, and investing, but also embrace eco-friendly business strategies like resource optimization, product life-cycle thinking, and waste reduction. Tailored training modules—delivered through workshops, mobile apps, or peer-to-peer mentoring—can bridge knowledge gaps and build confidence among borrowers. Financial literacy programs that integrate sustainability topics ensure that entrepreneurs make informed decisions, access appropriate green technologies, and scale their businesses responsibly. Ultimately, such education equips individuals and communities with the tools to create resilient, regenerative, and financially viable enterprises, reinforcing the impact of microfinance on both economic inclusion and environmental sustainability.

- **Innovative Loan Products** – To effectively support the transition to a circular economy, microfinance institutions must design tailored financial products that meet the unique needs of green and circular enterprises. Traditional loan models often fail to account for the longer return-on-investment cycles or upfront capital required for sustainable technologies and practices. By offering specialized green loans, MFIs can empower entrepreneurs to invest in eco-friendly equipment, renewable energy solutions, recycling operations, and sustainable raw materials. These products can include flexible repayment terms, grace periods, performance-based incentives, or lower interest rates for environmentally beneficial projects. Additionally, bundling loans with technical assistance or capacity-building programs can enhance borrowers' ability to implement and manage circular business models effectively. Impact-linked financing—where favorable terms are provided for achieving specific environmental or social outcomes—can further align financial incentives with sustainability goals. Through such innovative lending approaches, microfinance can play a pivotal role in catalyzing inclusive, scalable, and climate-resilient entrepreneurship at the grassroots level.
- **Public-Private Partnerships** – Public-private partnerships (PPPs) play a critical role in amplifying the reach and effectiveness of microfinance in advancing circular economy initiatives. By fostering collaborations between MFIs, government bodies, international development agencies, and private sector stakeholders, PPPs can unlock the financial, technical, and policy support needed to scale green entrepreneurship. Governments can provide subsidies, credit guarantees, or regulatory incentives that reduce the risk for MFIs lending to circular businesses. Meanwhile, private corporations and NGOs can offer market access, technology transfer, and training programs to build the capacity of micro-entrepreneurs. International organizations and development banks often act as catalysts by supplying funding, research, and impact frameworks that guide sustainable investment. These multi-stakeholder alliances are particularly effective in addressing systemic challenges—such as infrastructure gaps, financial exclusion, and climate vulnerability—while ensuring that microfinance solutions are aligned with national sustainability goals and global climate commitments. By working in concert, PPPs can create a supportive ecosystem where microfinance becomes a transformative driver of inclusive and

regenerative development.

Conclusion

Microfinance is a powerful tool in promoting the circular economy, offering social, economic, and environmental benefits. By fostering sustainable enterprises and financial inclusion, it drives economic growth while preserving resources for future generations. Strengthening microfinance frameworks will further enhance its role in building a resilient and inclusive circular economy.

CHAPTER SEVEN

A study on key indicators for job satisfaction in india

Author: Om Prakash Singh, Research Scholar at Jai Prakash University Chhapra Bihar

Abstract:

Job satisfaction is a crucial determinant of employee performance, organizational success, and overall well-being in the workforce. In India, where the labor market is diverse and rapidly evolving, understanding the key indicators of job satisfaction is vital for employers, policymakers, and researchers aiming to improve productivity, retention, and employee engagement. This study investigates the critical factors influencing job satisfaction among Indian employees across various sectors and industries.

Using a combination of quantitative and qualitative research methods, this study identifies and analyzes the key indicators of job satisfaction in the Indian context, including salary and benefits, work-life balance, career advancement opportunities, job security, management and leadership quality, and organizational culture. The research also explores the role of socio-demographic factors such as age, gender, education, and geographic location in shaping employees' job satisfaction levels.

The findings reveal that salary and work-life balance are among the most significant factors influencing job satisfaction in India, with employees prioritizing fair compensation and the ability to balance personal and professional commitments. Additionally, opportunities for career growth and the quality of leadership within organizations emerge as strong determinants of satisfaction, particularly for younger employees and those in metropolitan areas. Job security, while important, shows a varying impact depending on the industry, with public sector employees expressing greater job satisfaction related to stability.

The study also highlights the growing importance of organizational culture, with employees increasingly valuing a positive, inclusive, and supportive work environment. However, challenges such as work-related stress, long working hours, and lack of adequate employee recognition continue to affect job satisfaction, particularly in the private sector.

By providing a comprehensive understanding of the key indicators of job satisfaction in India, this study contributes valuable insights for organizations to enhance employee morale, improve retention, and foster a productive and engaged workforce, ultimately supporting the country's economic growth and development.

Introduction

Job satisfaction is a crucial factor that significantly influences employee productivity, organizational commitment, retention rates, and overall workplace morale. In the Indian context, where the workforce is highly diverse across sectors such as IT, manufacturing, services, and agriculture, understanding what drives job satisfaction is both complex and essential. Cultural values, socioeconomic conditions, generational differences, and industry-specific dynamics all shape how Indian employees perceive their jobs. As India continues to experience rapid economic growth and labor market transformation, gauging job satisfaction becomes even more vital for businesses aiming to attract and retain talent in a competitive environment. This study delves into the key determinants of job satisfaction among Indian employees—including work-life balance, compensation, job security, career growth opportunities, management practices, and organizational culture—with the goal of offering actionable insights for employers and policymakers seeking to foster healthier, more engaging, and sustainable workplaces.

Key Indicators of Job Satisfaction

Work-Life Balance is one of the most significant contributors to job satisfaction among Indian employees, especially in today's fast-paced and digitally connected work culture. With the rise of remote work, extended working hours, and high performance expectations—particularly in sectors like IT, finance, and services—many professionals struggle to maintain a healthy equilibrium between professional responsibilities and personal well-being. For working parents, caregivers, and women professionals, the challenge is often compounded by societal expectations and domestic duties. Employees who experience a lack of flexibility or excessive work pressure are more prone to stress, burnout, and disengagement. On the other hand, organizations that promote flexible work arrangements, encourage time off, and foster a culture that respects personal time often enjoy higher levels of employee morale, loyalty, and productivity. In the Indian context, where family ties and personal commitments hold significant value, ensuring work-life balance is not just an HR strategy—it is a core aspect of creating humane and high-performing workplaces.

- Flexible working hours and remote work options.
- Adequate paid leaves and mental health support.
- Reduced workplace stress and burnout.

Salary and Benefits Compensation remains a fundamental driver of job satisfaction across all sectors in India. For many employees, salary is directly linked to financial stability, social status, and perceived value within an organization. In a country with significant income disparities and a rising cost of living—especially in metropolitan areas—fair and competitive pay is essential for maintaining workforce motivation and retention. Beyond the base salary, benefits such as health insurance, retirement plans, bonuses, paid leave, and performance incentives contribute to an employee's overall sense of security and satisfaction. In recent years, forward-thinking companies have also introduced non-monetary perks like wellness programs, childcare support, and flexible work allowances to attract and retain top talent. While salary expectations may vary based on industry, experience, and location, transparent compensation structures and regular reviews are universally appreciated. Ultimately, when employees feel that their efforts are recognized and rewarded appropriately, it leads to greater loyalty, engagement, and long-term organizational commitment.

- Competitive compensation aligned with industry standards.
- Health insurance, retirement benefits, and performance-based incentives.
- Opportunities for financial growth and job security.

Career Growth and Development Opportunities for career advancement and professional development are critical to job satisfaction, particularly among India's large and ambitious young workforce. Employees value clear pathways for growth—whether through promotions, skill-building programs, or lateral mobility within the organization. In a rapidly evolving job market driven by technology and globalization, individuals are increasingly seeking roles that not only offer stability but also facilitate continuous learning and career progression. Lack of upward mobility, stagnant roles, or limited access to training often result in dissatisfaction and high attrition, especially in sectors like IT, BPO, and banking. Conversely, companies that invest in leadership development, mentorship programs, and upskilling initiatives tend to foster a more engaged and motivated workforce. In the Indian context, where educational attainment is often seen as a stepping stone to success, aligning organizational growth strategies with employee aspirations can yield significant benefits—both for talent retention and for building a future-ready workforce.

- Training programs, skill enhancement initiatives, and promotions.
- Clear career progression paths within organizations.
- Opportunities for learning through mentorship and professional development.

Work Environment and Organizational Culture A positive work environment and supportive organizational culture are foundational to job satisfaction in India's diverse professional landscape. Beyond tangible elements like office infrastructure and safety, the psychological atmosphere—shaped by leadership style, peer relationships, communication practices, and inclusivity—plays a significant role in how employees perceive their workplace. Indian employees increasingly value respectful, transparent, and collaborative environments where ideas are heard and contributions are recognized. Toxic cultures marked by micromanagement, favoritism, or rigid hierarchies can severely undermine morale and productivity. In contrast, organizations that promote open communication, innovation, mutual respect, and employee well-being often enjoy higher engagement and loyalty. With growing awareness around mental health and work-life integration, modern Indian professionals are also looking for empathetic leadership and a culture that prioritizes people as much as performance. Cultivating such environments not only boosts individual satisfaction but also drives organizational resilience and long-term success.

- Supportive management and collaborative team dynamics.
- Workplace diversity, inclusivity, and ethical business practices.
- Recognition and appreciation of employee contributions.

Job Security and Stability Job security remains one of the most deeply valued aspects of employment among Indian workers, often influencing career decisions more than perks or even higher salaries. In a country where economic uncertainties, industry disruptions, and informal employment are prevalent, stable jobs provide a sense of financial safety, social respect, and long-term planning capacity. This is especially true for middle- and lower-income segments, as well as for older employees or those supporting extended families. Sectors like government services, public sector enterprises, and large private corporations continue to attract talent due to their reputation for long-term employment and structured growth. Conversely, rising gig work, start-up volatility, and frequent layoffs in certain industries like tech have created anxiety around job continuity. Organizations that offer clear employment contracts, transparent policies, and proactive communication during downturns tend to instill greater trust and commitment among their employees. In the Indian context, where employment is closely linked with family welfare and social stability, fostering job security is essential for building a satisfied and resilient workforce.

- Long-term employment prospects and reduced job uncertainty.
- Fair labor practices and adherence to employment laws.
- Industry stability and economic factors influencing job security.

Employee Engagement and Autonomy Employee engagement and autonomy are increasingly recognized as powerful determinants of job satisfaction in modern Indian workplaces. Engagement goes beyond mere task completion—it involves emotional and intellectual involvement in one's work. When employees feel connected to the organization's goals and believe their contributions matter, they are more likely to be productive, innovative, and loyal. Autonomy—having the freedom to make decisions, manage tasks, and use discretion in daily responsibilities—further enhances this sense of ownership. In India, where traditional top-down management structures have often limited decision-making at lower levels, there is a growing shift toward empowering employees through participatory leadership, flexible work models, and collaborative cultures. Millennials and Gen Z workers, in particular, expect roles that offer purpose, voice, and freedom to shape their work. Companies that foster open feedback systems, recognize initiative, and reduce micromanagement tend to see higher motivation, lower turnover, and a more dynamic workplace culture. In essence, when employees are trusted and actively involved, satisfaction and performance naturally follow.

- Participation in decision-making processes.
- Sense of ownership and control over job responsibilities.
- Encouragement of creativity and innovation at work.

Workplace Relationships and Communication Strong interpersonal relationships and effective communication within the workplace are vital to fostering a positive and satisfying work experience. In the Indian cultural context—where community, hierarchy, and mutual respect hold significant value—the quality of interactions between colleagues, supervisors, and teams can greatly impact job satisfaction. Trust, empathy, and approachability in workplace relationships help reduce stress, build cooperation, and encourage knowledge sharing. Clear, respectful communication—both formal and informal—ensures that employees feel heard, understood, and included in decision-making processes. Conversely, poor communication or interpersonal conflicts can lead to misunderstandings, low morale, and disengagement. Organizations that encourage open dialogue, provide conflict resolution mechanisms, and promote team-building activities often see stronger collaboration and employee loyalty. Especially in India's diverse and multilingual work environments, fostering inclusive communication styles and cross-cultural awareness is key to building harmonious and productive workplaces.

- Effective communication between employees and management.
- Healthy relationships with colleagues and superiors.
- Conflict resolution mechanisms and grievance redressal systems.

Research Methodology

This study employs a mixed-methods approach, combining both quantitative and qualitative research techniques to provide a comprehensive understanding of the factors influencing job satisfaction among employees in India. The methodology was designed to capture insights across industries, age groups, and organizational levels.

Findings and Implications

The study revealed that job satisfaction among Indian employees is influenced by a blend of tangible and intangible factors, with work-life balance emerging as the most critical. Employees across sectors expressed a growing need for flexible work arrangements, especially in metro areas and technology-driven industries. Salary and benefits continue to be vital, particularly for early-career professionals; however, experienced employees showed a stronger inclination toward job security and career advancement. Limited opportunities for professional growth and upskilling were frequently cited as sources of dissatisfaction, pointing to the need for more structured development programs. Furthermore, organizational culture and leadership style were found to have a profound effect on employee morale—transparent communication, inclusive policies, and participative management significantly boosted job satisfaction levels.

Another important finding was the role of autonomy and engagement. Employees who felt empowered to make decisions and contribute meaningfully to their work demonstrated higher commitment and productivity. Similarly, positive workplace relationships, built on trust and collaboration, played a key role in creating a supportive environment. On the other hand, concerns about job security were more prominent in the private and startup sectors, where frequent restructuring led to heightened anxiety. These findings underscore the importance of sector-specific strategies and the need for organizations to adopt a holistic approach to employee well-being.

The implications are clear: organizations must re-evaluate their human resource strategies to better align with employee expectations. This includes designing flexible policies, fostering inclusive leadership, providing continuous learning opportunities, and strengthening the employee value proposition beyond financial incentives. For policymakers, the results highlight the importance of labor reforms and public-private partnerships to improve workplace standards, especially in India's informal and MSME sectors. Overall, enhancing job satisfaction is not only essential for workforce retention but also for driving organizational performance and national economic growth.

Preliminary research suggests that:

- IT and corporate sector employees value work-life balance and career growth.
- Manufacturing and blue-collar workers prioritize job security and fair wages.
- Healthcare and education professionals focus on work environment and benefits.

Conclusion

Job satisfaction in India is influenced by multiple factors ranging from salary to workplace culture. Organizations that prioritize employee well-being, career growth, and fair compensation can foster a more motivated and productive workforce. Future studies can focus on sector-specific job satisfaction trends and the impact of changing work dynamics, such as the rise of remote work and gig economy jobs.

CHAPTER EIGHT

An exploratory study on digital networking for self help groups in India

Author: Vishal Kanodia, Research Scholar at Jai Prakash University Chhapra Bihar

Abstract:

Self-Help Groups (SHGs) have emerged as a key mechanism for empowering marginalized communities in India, particularly women, by fostering financial independence, skill development, and social cohesion. With the increasing penetration of digital technologies in rural and semi-urban areas, there is a growing interest in leveraging digital networking tools to enhance the effectiveness and reach of SHGs. This exploratory study examines the role of digital networking in strengthening SHGs in India, focusing on its potential to improve communication, financial management, market access, and overall group sustainability.

The research employs a mixed-methods approach, combining surveys and interviews with SHG members, facilitators, and local NGOs to gather insights on the adoption and impact of digital tools within SHG operations. Key areas of investigation include the use of mobile applications, social media platforms, digital payments, and online training modules to improve the functionality and productivity of SHGs. The study also explores the barriers to digital adoption, such as lack of digital literacy, limited internet connectivity, and resistance to technological change.

Findings from the study highlight several benefits of digital networking for SHGs. Digital tools enable more efficient financial record-keeping, better communication between members, and improved access to markets for selling

products, thus enhancing the economic opportunities of SHG members. Additionally, online platforms facilitate skill development through digital learning resources and webinars, fostering greater knowledge-sharing and capacity building. The study also identifies challenges, including the need for targeted digital literacy programs and infrastructure development in remote areas.

This research suggests that integrating digital networking into the functioning of SHGs can significantly empower women, improve their entrepreneurial ventures, and increase their participation in the broader economy. It also emphasizes the importance of creating a supportive ecosystem, involving government agencies, NGOs, and technology providers, to overcome existing barriers and promote digital inclusion within SHGs.

In conclusion, digital networking has the potential to transform SHGs in India, enhancing their sustainability, outreach, and impact. However, a holistic approach is required to ensure that the benefits of digital technologies are accessible to all members, particularly in rural and underserved regions.

Introduction

Self-Help Groups (SHGs) have played a significant role in empowering rural and marginalized communities in India by promoting financial inclusion, entrepreneurship, and social development. The integration of digital networking tools has further enhanced the effectiveness of SHGs by facilitating communication, knowledge sharing, and access to financial and market opportunities. This study explores the role of digital networking in strengthening SHGs in India and the challenges and opportunities associated with it.

Role of Digital Networking in SHGs

Digital networking plays a transformative role in enhancing the efficiency, reach, and impact of Self-Help Groups (SHGs) across India. By leveraging mobile technology, social media platforms, and digital financial tools, SHGs are now able to communicate more effectively, share knowledge, access markets, and manage finances with greater transparency. Online platforms facilitate regular interactions among members, enable peer learning, and foster collaboration with NGOs, financial institutions, and government agencies. Digital payment systems and online banking have made savings and credit operations more secure and accessible, particularly for women in rural areas. Additionally, digital literacy empowers SHG members to promote their products through e-commerce and social media, expanding income-generating opportunities beyond local markets. Overall, digital networking strengthens the organizational capabilities of SHGs, fosters social inclusion, and accelerates grassroots economic development.

Digital networking has transformed the way SHGs operate, providing them with various advantages, including:

1. Enhanced Communication and Collaboration

Digital networking has significantly improved communication and collaboration within and among Self-Help Groups (SHGs). Mobile messaging apps, video conferencing tools, and social media platforms allow members to stay connected, share updates, and coordinate activities in real-time, regardless of geographical barriers. This connectivity has empowered SHG members—especially women in rural and remote areas—to voice opinions, participate in decision-making, and collectively solve challenges. It also facilitates better coordination with external stakeholders, such as NGOs, microfinance institutions, and government bodies, leading to improved access to training, funding, and resources. By fostering an environment of continuous interaction and mutual support, digital tools strengthen the social fabric of SHGs and enhance their ability to function as cohesive, empowered units.

Would you like the next point now (e.g., "2. Financial Inclusion and Transparency")?

4o

- Use of WhatsApp, Facebook, and other social media platforms for group discussions.
- Digital platforms enabling real-time interaction among SHG members and stakeholders.

2. Access to Financial Services

Digital networking has significantly broadened the access of Self-Help Groups (SHGs) to various financial services, enabling them to overcome traditional barriers associated with the formal banking system. Through mobile banking, digital wallets, and online microfinance platforms, SHGs can now perform transactions, manage savings, and access credit more easily and securely. Digital tools have also facilitated direct disbursements of loans and subsidies, reducing dependency on intermediaries and ensuring faster, more transparent financial support. In addition, digital platforms offer SHGs the opportunity to build a digital credit history, which is essential for accessing larger loans and expanding business ventures. By incorporating digital payment systems, SHGs can engage in cashless transactions, enhancing transparency and reducing the risks of theft or mismanagement of funds. Furthermore, these digital platforms often provide features such as financial literacy programs, helping members better understand and manage their finances, ultimately contributing to the overall financial inclusion of marginalized communities.

- Mobile banking and digital payment systems improving financial transactions.
- Digital lending platforms enabling access to microfinance and credit facilities.

3. Market Linkages and Entrepreneurship

Digital networking has opened up new avenues for Self-Help Groups (SHGs) to access broader markets and create entrepreneurial opportunities. By leveraging e-commerce platforms, social media, and digital marketing tools, SHGs can now promote and sell their products to a global audience, transcending local market limitations. Online marketplaces, such as Amazon, Flipkart, and regional platforms, allow SHGs to showcase handmade crafts, organic produce, and other local goods, reaching customers far beyond their immediate geographic area. Additionally, digital networking provides valuable insights into market trends and consumer preferences, allowing SHGs to adapt their offerings to meet demand. These connections also facilitate collaborations with larger businesses, enabling SHGs to become suppliers or partners in value chains. Through digital platforms, SHGs can access training on entrepreneurship, product development, and business management, which strengthens their ability to scale operations, innovate, and sustain long-term growth. This digital shift empowers members to become entrepreneurs in their own right, creating new sources of income and economic independence for individuals, especially women.

- E-commerce platforms allowing SHG products to reach wider markets.
- Online networking facilitating partnerships and collaborations with businesses.

4. Capacity Building and Skill Development

Digital networking plays a pivotal role in enhancing the capacity and skills of Self-Help Groups (SHGs), empowering members with the knowledge and tools necessary for personal and professional growth. Online training programs, webinars, and e-learning platforms provide SHG members with access to a wealth of resources in areas such as financial management, entrepreneurship, digital literacy, and vocational skills. These digital learning opportunities help bridge the knowledge gap and equip members with skills relevant to the modern economy. Additionally, online platforms often offer certification programs that enhance the credibility of SHG members' expertise, increasing their chances of securing funding, partnerships, or employment opportunities. By connecting SHGs with industry experts and trainers through digital networks, members also benefit from real-time mentoring and peer-to-peer learning. As a result, digital networking fosters a culture of continuous improvement, enabling SHGs to become more self-sufficient, resilient, and adaptable in an ever-evolving economic landscape.

- E-learning resources for entrepreneurship and financial literacy.
- Webinars and virtual training sessions conducted by NGOs and government bodies.

Challenges in Digital Adoption by SHGs

The adoption of digital technologies by Self-Help Groups (SHGs) faces several challenges that hinder their progress. A major barrier is the lack of digital literacy among SHG members, especially in rural areas, where many may not have the skills or exposure to modern technology. Limited access to devices, poor internet connectivity, and unreliable infrastructure in remote areas further complicate digital adoption. Additionally, cultural resistance and financial constraints prevent SHG members from fully embracing technology, as the costs associated with digital tools, such as devices, internet plans, and software, can be prohibitive. The lack of adequate training and technical support also limits their ability to effectively use digital platforms. Moreover, concerns over privacy and security, as well as a general resistance to change, can deter members from adopting digital solutions. Language barriers and limited awareness of the benefits of digital tools also hinder widespread adoption. Finally, the absence of supportive policies or a fragmented digital ecosystem adds to the complexity of integrating technology into SHGs. Overcoming these challenges requires a combination of digital literacy programs, affordable technology, community-based support, and government intervention to ensure sustainable and meaningful digital adoption.

Despite its potential, digital networking in SHGs faces several barriers:

1. Digital Literacy and Accessibility

Digital Literacy and Accessibility are two fundamental challenges in the digital adoption process for Self-Help Groups (SHGs). Digital literacy refers to the ability to effectively and confidently use digital tools and platforms, which is often lacking in rural and marginalized communities where SHGs are prevalent. Many members may not have basic skills in using smartphones, computers, or navigating the internet, making it difficult for them to engage with digital platforms designed for financial management, communication, or education. Without proper training and support, they may feel intimidated or unable to make full use of technology.

Accessibility, on the other hand, pertains to the physical and infrastructural resources needed to access digital tools. Many SHGs operate in areas where access to reliable internet connectivity, electricity, and digital devices is limited. In rural and remote locations, poor network coverage and power shortages can significantly hinder the use of digital tools, further widening the digital divide. Even when devices are available, they may not be affordable for SHGs, which often operate with limited resources. These dual challenges of digital literacy and accessibility must be addressed through targeted initiatives like digital education programs, affordable technology solutions, and improvements in infrastructure to make digital tools more inclusive and usable for SHGs.

- Limited digital skills among SHG members, especially in rural areas.
- Inadequate internet connectivity and smartphone penetration.

2. Affordability and Infrastructure Issues

Affordability and Infrastructure Issues are significant challenges faced by Self-Help Groups (SHGs) when adopting digital technologies. Many SHGs operate in economically constrained environments, where the cost of digital tools such as smartphones, computers, and internet connections is a major barrier. The upfront costs of purchasing devices and ongoing expenses for data plans or subscriptions can be unaffordable for SHG members, who often come from low-income backgrounds. This makes it difficult for them to invest in the necessary technology to enhance their operations or gain access to digital financial services, educational resources, or business tools.

Alongside affordability, infrastructure issues further complicate digital adoption. In rural or remote areas, where many SHGs are based, unreliable electricity and poor internet connectivity are common challenges. Even if SHG members can afford devices, a lack of stable power supply or internet access can make it difficult to use digital tools effectively. Slow internet speeds and intermittent service can hinder online transactions, communications, or access to digital platforms, reducing the overall usefulness of technology. To overcome these challenges, there is a need for government and private sector investment in affordable, accessible digital solutions, alongside infrastructure improvements like better internet connectivity and reliable power supply in underserved areas.

- High costs of digital devices and data services.
- Lack of proper digital infrastructure in remote regions.

3. Cybersecurity and Data Privacy Concerns

Cybersecurity and Data Privacy Concerns are critical issues that pose significant challenges to the digital adoption of Self-Help Groups (SHGs). Many SHG members may not be fully aware of the risks associated with using digital platforms, such as identity theft, fraud, or data breaches. These risks can deter SHG members from embracing digital tools, particularly when handling sensitive financial information or personal data. Without a clear understanding of how to protect their data, SHG members may feel vulnerable to cyberattacks or misuse of their information.

Additionally, many SHGs lack the technical expertise to ensure their digital systems are secure. This can make them targets for cybercriminals, especially when they engage in online transactions or share information over unsecured networks. The absence of robust cybersecurity measures, such as encryption, secure payment gateways, and data protection protocols, increases the chances of their data being compromised. To address these concerns, it is essential to provide SHGs with digital literacy training that includes cybersecurity best practices, secure platform recommendations, and guidance on data privacy laws. Furthermore, digital platforms designed for SHGs should be built with strong security features to protect sensitive information, fostering trust and encouraging greater digital engagement.

- Risks associated with online financial transactions and digital fraud.
- Lack of awareness about data protection and secure digital practices.

Government and NGO Initiatives

Government and NGO Initiatives play a vital role in addressing the challenges faced by Self-Help Groups (SHGs) in adopting digital technologies. Both government bodies and non-governmental organizations (NGOs) have been instrumental in supporting digital inclusion through various programs and interventions aimed at improving access to technology, building digital literacy, and providing necessary infrastructure.

Governments often launch initiatives focused on expanding internet access and improving digital infrastructure in rural and underserved areas. Programs such as the Digital India campaign in India or similar initiatives in other countries have worked to bring affordable internet services, subsidized devices, and digital literacy training to marginalized communities. These programs are designed to bridge the digital divide by providing SHGs with the tools and resources needed to embrace technology. Additionally, governments may provide financial incentives or subsidies for SHGs to purchase digital devices, thereby making them more affordable.

NGOs also play a crucial role by offering capacity-building programs to enhance digital literacy and awareness among SHG members. They often organize workshops, provide hands-on training, and develop digital platforms tailored to the specific needs of SHGs, ensuring that the tools are user-friendly and accessible. NGOs may also collaborate with local governments to address infrastructure gaps, such as installing internet connectivity in remote areas or providing solar-powered solutions to overcome electricity issues.

Moreover, both governments and NGOs can assist in creating a supportive policy environment that encourages the use of digital tools for financial inclusion, business development, and educational advancement. By working together, government bodies and NGOs can help SHGs overcome barriers to digital adoption and empower them to leverage technology for improved socio-economic outcomes.

Several initiatives have been undertaken to promote digital networking among SHGs:

- **National Rural Livelihoods Mission (NRLM)** – Encouraging digital financial literacy and online networking among SHG members.
- **Digital Saksharta Abhiyan (DISHA)** – Providing digital literacy training to rural communities.
- **NGO-Led Training Programs** – Many NGOs are implementing digital empowerment projects for SHGs.

Future Prospects and Recommendations

To maximize the benefits of digital networking for SHGs, the following strategies can be adopted:

1. **Digital Literacy Training Programs** – Digital Literacy Training Programs are crucial for the successful digital adoption of Self-Help Groups (SHGs), and both government and private stakeholders should invest in initiatives aimed at building digital skills. For many SHG members, especially in rural and marginalized communities, a lack of basic digital knowledge is a significant barrier to adopting technology. By offering targeted training programs, these stakeholders can empower SHG members to navigate digital platforms confidently, enabling them to improve their operations, manage finances, and access new opportunities.

   Government investment in digital literacy programs can take the form of nationwide campaigns, subsidies for training institutions, or partnerships with educational organizations to provide courses tailored to the specific needs of SHGs. Programs like Digital India in India, for example, have been designed to promote digital literacy and make technology more accessible, especially in rural areas. Local governments can also collaborate with educational institutions to create training hubs or mobile training units that travel to underserved areas, providing on-the-ground digital education.

   Private stakeholders, such as tech companies and NGOs, can play a complementary role by providing specialized training tools and resources. They can collaborate with governments or community organizations to offer free or low-cost digital literacy courses, workshops, and webinars focused on skills like using smartphones, managing online banking, understanding cybersecurity, or leveraging digital platforms for marketing and sales. Additionally, private companies can develop and distribute easy-to-use digital tools that are tailored to the needs of SHGs, ensuring that the platforms they adopt are accessible and user-friendly.

Moreover, both sectors can work together to ensure that training programs are sustainable and scalable, integrating them into community development efforts and offering continuous support as SHGs transition to digital tools. By building digital literacy, SHG members gain confidence, improve their productivity, and become better equipped to navigate the digital economy, ultimately strengthening their organizations and enhancing their socio-economic outcomes.

2. **Affordable Internet and Device Accessibility** – Affordable Internet and Device Accessibility are key components in enabling the digital transformation of Self-Help Groups (SHGs), especially in rural areas. One of the major barriers to digital adoption in these regions is the lack of affordable and reliable internet connectivity, coupled with the high cost of digital devices. Expanding rural broadband infrastructure and subsidizing digital devices for SHG members are essential steps to overcoming these challenges.

Governments, in collaboration with private sector players, should prioritize the expansion of rural broadband infrastructure to ensure that SHGs have access to fast, reliable, and affordable internet services. By investing in improved network connectivity in remote and underserved areas, governments can bridge the digital divide, enabling SHG members to access online platforms for financial services, training, business development, and communication. Public-private partnerships could play a crucial role in accelerating this process, with internet service providers offering discounted rates or rural-focused packages to make connectivity more affordable for SHGs.

Simultaneously, subsidizing digital devices—such as smartphones, tablets, or laptops—can further lower the entry barriers for SHG members. Many SHG members come from low-income backgrounds and may struggle to afford even basic devices required for digital adoption. Governments and NGOs can implement programs that either provide discounted or free devices to SHG members or offer financial assistance to help purchase them. Private companies could also offer discounted devices tailored to the needs of SHGs, with easy-to-use interfaces and pre-installed apps relevant to their operations. Additionally, collaborations with local retailers and tech companies to create affordable device financing schemes would enable SHGs to acquire technology without significant upfront costs.

By addressing both internet accessibility and device affordability, these initiatives can provide SHGs with the necessary tools to embrace digital technology, improve their operational efficiency, access financial resources, and connect with markets or service providers more effectively. This, in turn, would help SHGs become more resilient, self-sustaining, and empowered to thrive in the digital age.

3. **Cybersecurity Awareness and Support Systems** – Cybersecurity Awareness and Support Systems are crucial for ensuring the safe and effective use of digital technologies by Self-Help Groups (SHGs). As SHGs increasingly engage with digital platforms for financial transactions, communication, and business management, they are exposed to various cyber threats, including fraud, identity theft, and data breaches. To protect SHG members and build their confidence in digital tools, establishing digital grievance redressal mechanisms and educating SHGs on safe digital practices is essential.

   Cybersecurity education should be a central part of digital literacy programs for SHGs. Members need to understand basic cybersecurity concepts such as recognizing phishing attacks, creating strong passwords, and protecting sensitive financial data. Regular workshops and training sessions on digital security should be organized by both government bodies and private sector stakeholders. These sessions can cover topics such as secure online transactions, the importance of encryption, and how to safeguard personal and financial information while using digital platforms.

   In addition to education, digital grievance redressal mechanisms are necessary to support SHG members when they face cybersecurity issues. Establishing clear channels through which members can report security concerns or incidents—such as fraud or unauthorized access to accounts—can help quickly resolve issues and prevent further harm. These mechanisms should include dedicated helplines, online support, or even local points of contact where SHG members can seek assistance. Governments and NGOs can work together to create these support systems, ensuring that SHGs feel confident that any cybersecurity issues they encounter will be addressed promptly and effectively.

   Furthermore, partnering with tech companies to provide ongoing technical support and security updates to the digital platforms used by SHGs can help mitigate risks. Regular audits, security upgrades, and monitoring can help prevent cyber threats from undermining the success of SHGs' digital initiatives.

By fostering cybersecurity awareness and offering robust support systems, SHGs can better protect themselves from digital threats while embracing the benefits of technology. Empowering SHG members with the knowledge and resources to stay safe online enhances their digital engagement, builds trust in digital platforms, and ensures the long-term success of their digital adoption.

4. **Integration with E-Governance Platforms** – Integration with E-Governance Platforms is a powerful strategy to enhance the digital adoption of Self-Help Groups (SHGs) and improve their access to essential government services, financial aid, and resources. Many governments have developed e-governance platforms to streamline public services and improve transparency, but SHGs often face challenges in accessing these services due to lack of awareness, digital literacy, or infrastructure. By linking SHGs with these platforms, governments can help ensure that SHGs can easily access the benefits of digital government services, including financial assistance, subsidies, training programs, and social welfare schemes.

   The integration of SHGs with e-governance platforms can provide a seamless process for accessing financial aid such as grants, low-interest loans, and subsidies. Many government schemes aimed at promoting women's empowerment, rural development, and poverty alleviation already exist, but SHGs may struggle to navigate the complex application processes or lack the digital tools required to apply. By simplifying access to these services through e-governance, SHGs can quickly apply for financial support, track the status of their applications, and ensure faster disbursement of funds. Moreover, linking SHGs with digital financial services such as digital banking, mobile wallets, and micro-insurance products can improve their financial inclusion, making it easier to save, invest, or get loans.

   Governments can also use e-governance platforms to offer training and capacity-building resources to SHGs, ensuring they are well-equipped to manage their finances, expand their businesses, or learn new skills. Digital platforms can host webinars, online courses, and workshops focused on improving business acumen, digital literacy, and entrepreneurship skills, empowering SHG members to thrive in a digital economy.

Furthermore, integrating SHGs into e-governance systems allows for greater transparency and accountability. By leveraging digital systems, SHGs can track the status of government programs and ensure that resources are being allocated and used efficiently. Real-time access to data can also help SHGs make informed decisions, plan their activities better, and collaborate more effectively with government agencies or other stakeholders.

To make this integration successful, governments must ensure that e-governance platforms are user-friendly, accessible, and inclusive. These platforms should be designed with the specific needs of SHGs in mind, including multi-language support, simplified interfaces, and mobile accessibility. Additionally, government initiatives should focus on building digital literacy among SHG members so they can effectively navigate these platforms.

By linking SHGs with digital government services, governments can significantly enhance the reach and impact of their welfare programs, support SHGs in their growth, and promote broader socio-economic development.

Conclusion

Digital networking has the potential to revolutionize SHGs in India by enhancing connectivity, financial inclusion, and market access. However, overcoming digital literacy barriers, infrastructure challenges, and cybersecurity concerns is crucial for its successful implementation. With collaborative efforts from the government, NGOs, and the private sector, digital networking can significantly empower SHGs, leading to economic and social progress in India.

CHAPTER NINE

Key Performance Indicators in hr analytics

Author: Dr. Alka Lalhall, Associate Professor at Central University of Himachal Pradesh

Co-Author: Rashmi Raj, Research Scholar at Mahatma Gandhi Central University, Bihar

Abstract:

Human Resources (HR) analytics has evolved into a critical tool for organizations seeking to optimize their workforce and improve decision-making processes. By leveraging data-driven insights, HR professionals can assess and enhance various aspects of employee performance, engagement, retention, and development. The use of Key Performance Indicators (KPIs) in HR analytics is essential to measure the effectiveness of HR initiatives, align them with organizational goals, and drive overall business performance.

This study explores the key performance indicators used in HR analytics, examining their role in tracking and evaluating workforce management strategies. Key areas of focus include recruitment efficiency, employee engagement, training and development, retention rates, productivity, and workforce diversity. The research investigates how these KPIs are employed across different industries and organizational sizes, highlighting best practices, challenges, and emerging trends in HR analytics.

The findings indicate that KPIs such as time-to-hire, cost-per-hire, employee turnover rate, absenteeism, employee satisfaction, and performance metrics are among the most commonly used indicators. Furthermore, the integration of advanced HR analytics tools, such as predictive modeling and data visualization, allows organizations to gain deeper insights into workforce dynamics and improve decision-making. The study also identifies the importance of aligning HR KPIs with broader business objectives, ensuring that

HR strategies contribute to organizational success.

Despite the benefits, challenges such as data quality, privacy concerns, and the need for skilled HR professionals to interpret analytics findings remain prevalent. Additionally, the study emphasizes the importance of fostering a data-driven culture within HR departments to maximize the potential of HR analytics.

In conclusion, KPIs in HR analytics are vital for optimizing HR functions, enhancing employee experiences, and driving business growth. As organizations increasingly rely on data to inform HR strategies, the effective use of these indicators will be crucial in shaping the future of workforce management and organizational development.

Introduction

Human Resource (HR) Analytics plays a critical role in measuring and improving workforce efficiency, engagement, and overall organizational success. By leveraging data and analytics, organizations can gain valuable insights into employee performance, retention, satisfaction, and other essential aspects of human capital management. Key Performance Indicators (KPIs) are fundamental to HR analytics, as they provide measurable data points that help HR professionals evaluate the effectiveness of their strategies and make data-driven decisions to enhance organizational outcomes.

The key KPIs in HR analytics can be categorized into several key areas, including workforce productivity, employee engagement, talent acquisition, retention, and learning and development.

Essential HR KPIs

Essential HR Key Performance Indicators (KPIs) are metrics used to measure and track the effectiveness of human resource strategies and initiatives within an organization. These KPIs help HR professionals make data-driven decisions to improve workforce efficiency, engagement, and organizational performance. Here are some of the most essential HR KPIs:

1. Employee Turnover Rate

Definition:

Employee turnover rate is a key performance indicator (KPI) that measures the percentage of employees who leave an organization over a specific period. This metric is crucial for assessing an organization's ability to retain talent and understanding the underlying reasons for departures. High turnover rates can signal problems within the organization, such as low employee satisfaction, inadequate compensation, or poor workplace culture.

Significance:

Employee turnover can be costly for organizations, both in terms of recruitment and training new staff, and in terms of the loss of institutional knowledge and productivity. Monitoring turnover helps organizations identify trends, assess the effectiveness of retention strategies, and implement improvements where necessary.

Why It's Important:

1. **Retention Issues:** A high turnover rate may indicate issues such as dissatisfaction with work conditions, management practices, or compensation.
2. **Recruitment and Training Costs:** High turnover means more hiring and training expenses, which can put a strain on the organization's budget.
3. **Employee Morale:** Frequent employee departures can negatively affect the morale of remaining employees, leading to lower engagement and productivity.
4. **Workplace Culture:** Understanding turnover patterns can help the organization evaluate the health of its workplace culture and leadership style.
5. **Predictive Tool:** Tracking turnover allows HR to identify at-risk employees or departments, and take proactive steps to improve retention.

- Measures the percentage of employees leaving an organization over a specific period.
- Formula: (Number of separations / Average number of employees) × 100.
- Helps identify retention issues and assess organizational stability.

2. Time to Hire

Definition:

Time to hire is the metric that tracks the number of days it takes to fill a job opening, from when the job requisition is approved to when the candidate accepts the offer. This KPI is crucial for assessing the efficiency and effectiveness of an organization's recruitment process.

Significance:
The time to hire directly impacts an organization's ability to meet business goals. A prolonged hiring process can lead to the loss of top candidates to competitors, increased recruitment costs, and delays in achieving team or organizational objectives. On the other hand, a swift and efficient hiring process helps attract top talent and ensures teams are adequately staffed, minimizing productivity gaps.

Why It's Important:

1. **Candidate Experience:** A long time to hire can frustrate candidates, leading to a poor candidate experience. Candidates may lose interest or accept offers from other companies if the process is too slow.
2. **Talent Acquisition Efficiency:** A quick hiring process suggests that the recruitment strategy is efficient, that HR teams are well-coordinated, and that the hiring process is smooth.
3. **Workforce Gaps:** Delays in hiring can result in unfilled positions, creating productivity gaps, increased workload for existing employees, and potential delays in business operations or projects.
4. **Cost of Vacancy:** The longer a position remains open, the more it costs the organization in terms of lost productivity and the additional time HR spends sourcing candidates.
5. **Attracting Top Talent:** Top candidates often have multiple job offers. A long hiring process may lead to the organization losing out on desirable candidates to more agile competitors.

- Tracks the duration taken to fill a vacant position.
- Reflects recruitment efficiency and process effectiveness.

3. Cost per Hire
Definition:
Cost per hire is a key performance indicator (KPI) that measures the total cost incurred by an organization to recruit and hire a new employee. This includes all expenses related to the recruitment process, such as advertising, agency fees, recruitment staff salaries, interview costs, background checks, and onboarding expenses. It is a vital metric for assessing the efficiency and financial effectiveness of the recruitment process.
Significance:
Cost per hire is important because it helps organizations evaluate how cost-

effective their recruitment strategies are. High costs per hire may indicate inefficiencies in the hiring process or reliance on expensive recruitment methods, while lower costs may suggest more efficient use of resources. By understanding this metric, companies can optimize their recruitment strategies, reduce unnecessary spending, and improve budget allocation for hiring.

Why It's Important:

1. **Budget Optimization:** By understanding the cost per hire, organizations can optimize recruitment spending, ensuring that money is spent efficiently while still attracting top talent.
2. **Recruitment Process Efficiency:** High costs per hire can point to inefficiencies, such as excessive reliance on recruitment agencies or expensive advertising channels. This information can help HR teams make necessary adjustments.
3. **Evaluation of Sourcing Channels:** This metric helps organizations assess which sourcing channels (job boards, referrals, agencies, etc.) are the most cost-effective for finding the right candidates.
4. **Strategic Planning:** Monitoring cost per hire allows HR and leadership teams to develop long-term recruitment strategies that balance costs and quality.
5. **Resource Allocation:** By analyzing this KPI, organizations can determine whether the recruitment budget is being allocated wisely, ensuring that investments in advertising, recruiting agencies, and other activities are providing the best return.

- Calculates the total cost incurred in hiring an employee.
- Includes expenses such as job advertisements, recruiter fees, and onboarding costs.
- Formula: (Total recruitment costs / Number of hires).

4. Employee Productivity Rate
Definition:
The employee productivity rate measures the efficiency of an employee in producing output relative to the amount of input or resources used. This can be evaluated by tracking specific outcomes such as sales, project completion, or other job-specific metrics over a defined period. It helps organizations assess the overall performance of their workforce and

determine the effectiveness of their employees in contributing to organizational goals.

Significance:

Employee productivity is one of the most important indicators of organizational success. High productivity rates are generally associated with higher profitability, efficient resource use, and improved competitiveness. By tracking this KPI, organizations can identify top performers, uncover areas for improvement, and make data-driven decisions regarding workforce management, training, and optimization.

Why It's Important:

1. **Operational Efficiency:** Understanding productivity helps optimize processes and workflows, ensuring that resources (time, labor, materials) are being used efficiently.
2. **Performance Evaluation:** Monitoring employee productivity allows HR to identify which employees or teams are performing well and which may need additional support, training, or resources.
3. **Revenue Generation:** High productivity often correlates with higher output, whether it's generating more sales, completing more projects, or achieving other key business outcomes.
4. **Cost Management:** By increasing productivity, organizations can often achieve the same or better results without adding additional labor costs, improving profitability.
5. **Employee Engagement and Motivation:** A productive workforce is often a result of high engagement levels, so tracking productivity can also serve as a barometer of employee satisfaction and morale.

- Assesses employee output relative to hours worked.
- Can be measured using performance evaluations, project completions, or revenue per employee.

5. Absenteeism Rate

Definition:

Absenteeism rate is a key performance indicator (KPI) that measures the percentage of workdays missed by employees due to illness, personal reasons, or other forms of unapproved absence. This metric is important because it helps organizations track how frequently employees are absent from work and can provide insights into employee engagement, health, job satisfaction, and the overall workplace environment.

Significance:

Absenteeism can have a significant impact on an organization's operations, leading to disruptions in productivity, increased workload for other employees, and higher costs due to temporary replacements or overtime. By monitoring absenteeism, HR teams can identify patterns and address underlying issues, such as health concerns, low morale, or management problems, that may be affecting employee attendance.

Why It's Important:

1. **Productivity Impact:** High absenteeism rates often lead to lost productivity as tasks may be delayed or reassigned, which can affect project timelines and team performance.
2. **Cost Implications:** Absenteeism can incur additional costs, including paying temporary staff, offering overtime, or compensating for lost work hours.
3. **Employee Engagement and Satisfaction:** Excessive absenteeism may indicate dissatisfaction with the work environment, job responsibilities, or work-life balance. It can also be a sign of poor employee morale.
4. **Health and Wellbeing:** Frequent absenteeism might be an indicator of workplace health and safety concerns, such as stress, burnout, or unhealthy work conditions.
5. **Predictive Value:** Tracking absenteeism trends can help identify potential problems early. For example, patterns of frequent short-term absenteeism may suggest burnout or a need for more flexible work arrangements.

- Measures the frequency of unplanned employee absences.
- Formula: (Total absence days / Total available workdays) × 100.
- Helps organizations address workplace engagement and wellness issues.

6. Employee Engagement Score

Definition:

The employee engagement score is a key performance indicator (KPI) that measures the level of emotional commitment and enthusiasm employees have toward their work and the organization. It is often determined through surveys or feedback tools where employees rate their job satisfaction, work environment, sense of purpose, and alignment with organizational goals.

This score reflects how engaged employees are in their roles and can provide insights into overall workforce morale and organizational health.

Significance:

Employee engagement is closely linked to productivity, retention, and overall business success. Highly engaged employees are more likely to be motivated, perform at higher levels, and remain with the organization longer. Low engagement, on the other hand, can result in reduced productivity, higher turnover rates, and lower morale across teams. By regularly measuring employee engagement, organizations can identify potential issues, enhance workplace culture, and take proactive steps to improve employee satisfaction and retention.

Why It's Important:

1. **Increased Productivity:** Engaged employees tend to be more motivated and put in extra effort, which directly contributes to higher productivity levels and better business outcomes.
2. **Lower Turnover Rates:** High engagement is a key factor in employee retention. Employees who are emotionally invested in their work are more likely to stay with the company, reducing turnover and the associated hiring and training costs.
3. **Improved Customer Satisfaction:** Engaged employees are often more enthusiastic about their work, which can translate into better customer service, higher quality of work, and improved customer satisfaction.
4. **Organizational Success:** Employee engagement is directly linked to organizational success. Engaged employees help foster a positive culture, which can result in innovation, collaboration, and overall organizational growth.
5. **Enhanced Employee Well-being:** A high engagement score often correlates with higher employee well-being, as engaged workers feel more connected to their job, have better work-life balance, and experience less stress and burnout.

- Evaluates employee motivation and satisfaction levels.
- Derived from surveys, feedback mechanisms, and Net Promoter Scores (NPS).
- Directly impacts productivity, retention, and overall morale.

7. Training Effectiveness and Learning Metrics

Definition:

Training effectiveness and learning metrics refer to the KPIs used to measure the success and impact of training and development programs within an organization. These metrics assess how well employees acquire new skills, improve performance, and apply knowledge gained from training to their daily tasks. By tracking these metrics, organizations can determine whether training initiatives are achieving their goals and contributing to overall organizational success.

Significance:

Effective training programs are crucial for enhancing employee skills, improving productivity, and fostering a culture of continuous learning. Measuring the effectiveness of these programs helps ensure that resources invested in training lead to tangible improvements in employee performance, engagement, and business outcomes. It also allows organizations to identify areas where training may need to be refined or adjusted for better results.

Why It's Important:

1. **Improved Employee Performance:** Training programs that are well-designed and effective can directly improve employee performance by equipping them with the necessary skills and knowledge to excel in their roles.
2. **Return on Investment (ROI):** Organizations invest significant resources in employee training, so measuring its effectiveness helps ensure that these investments yield measurable benefits in terms of productivity, quality, and business results.
3. **Skill Development:** Training effectiveness metrics can help track the development of key skills and competencies, ensuring that employees are prepared for current and future job demands.
4. **Employee Satisfaction and Retention:** Employees who feel that they are receiving valuable training opportunities are more likely to feel engaged, satisfied, and committed to the organization, which can improve retention rates.
5. **Alignment with Organizational Goals:** Measuring the effectiveness of training ensures that programs are aligned with broader organizational objectives and help achieve strategic goals.

- Measures the impact of employee training programs.

- Includes training completion rates, knowledge retention, and post-training performance improvement.

8. Diversity and Inclusion Metrics

Definition:

Diversity and inclusion (D&I) metrics are key performance indicators (KPIs) used to measure the success of initiatives aimed at promoting diversity, equity, and inclusion within an organization. These metrics help assess how well the organization is fostering a diverse and inclusive workplace where employees of all backgrounds feel valued, respected, and supported.

Diversity metrics typically focus on the representation of different demographic groups (e.g., gender, race, ethnicity, age, disability, sexual orientation) in the workforce. Inclusion metrics assess the work environment, such as whether employees feel included, valued, and have equal opportunities for advancement.

Significance:

Diversity and inclusion are crucial for fostering a workplace culture that embraces different perspectives, experiences, and backgrounds. A diverse workforce can lead to more creativity, innovation, and better decision-making. Inclusion ensures that all employees feel empowered, which leads to higher engagement, retention, and overall organizational performance. Measuring D&I helps organizations track their progress in these areas and identify where improvements are needed.

Why It's Important:

1. **Improved Innovation and Creativity:** A diverse workforce brings a variety of perspectives, which leads to creative solutions, better problem-solving, and innovative ideas.
2. **Higher Employee Engagement:** When employees feel included and valued, they are more likely to be engaged, productive, and committed to the organization.
3. **Better Decision-Making:** A diverse team can offer broader insights, which helps improve decision-making, reduce biases, and avoid groupthink.
4. **Talent Acquisition and Retention:** Organizations that prioritize diversity and inclusion attract a wider pool of talent and are better able to retain diverse employees, reducing turnover rates.

5. **Legal and Ethical Responsibility:** Ensuring diversity and inclusion can help organizations comply with regulations and contribute to a fair and equitable work environment.

- Tracks workforce diversity in terms of gender, ethnicity, and representation.
- Ensures equitable opportunities and compliance with diversity policies.

9. Compensation Competitiveness Index

Definition:

The Compensation Competitiveness Index (CCI) is a key performance indicator (KPI) used to assess how competitive an organization's compensation structure is compared to the broader labor market or industry standards. The CCI is designed to measure whether the organization is offering competitive salaries and benefits that attract and retain top talent while ensuring internal equity.

The CCI typically compares an organization's pay levels for similar roles (across various job functions) against market benchmarks. These benchmarks can come from industry reports, salary surveys, and compensation databases. A higher CCI indicates that an organization is paying at or above market rate, while a lower CCI may suggest that the organization is falling behind in compensation, which could impact recruitment and employee retention.

Significance:

Compensation plays a critical role in employee satisfaction, motivation, and retention. If an organization offers below-market salaries, it may struggle to attract qualified talent and may face higher turnover rates. On the other hand, offering competitive compensation ensures that employees feel valued and motivated to stay with the company, improving organizational performance. The CCI helps HR departments make data-driven decisions about salary adjustments, bonus structures, and other benefits to stay competitive in the labor market.

Why It's Important:

1. **Talent Acquisition:** Competitive compensation helps attract top-tier talent from the labor market. If an organization does not offer attractive salaries, it may lose out on qualified candidates.

2. **Employee Retention:** Offering competitive pay is one of the most important factors in retaining employees. If employees perceive that their pay is lower than industry standards, they may seek better opportunities elsewhere.

3. **Market Positioning:** The CCI helps an organization understand where it stands in comparison to other companies in the same industry or geographic location. It allows the organization to remain competitive in terms of compensation packages.

4. **Internal Equity:** The CCI ensures that employees are paid fairly within the organization based on their roles, skills, and experience relative to the market, helping to prevent wage disparities and fostering a sense of fairness.

5. **Employee Satisfaction:** Employees who feel they are compensated fairly and competitively are more likely to be satisfied with their jobs, leading to higher morale and productivity.

- Compares employee salaries with industry benchmarks.
- Helps in retaining top talent and maintaining competitive pay structures.

10. Promotion Rate and Internal Mobility
Definition:

Promotion Rate refers to the percentage of employees who are promoted within an organization over a specific period. This metric tracks the rate at which employees move up the organizational hierarchy or take on more senior roles.

Internal Mobility refers to the movement of employees within the organization, including promotions, lateral moves, and transfers to different departments or roles. This metric is concerned with the extent to which employees are provided opportunities to grow, develop, and advance within the company without seeking employment elsewhere.

Together, promotion rate and internal mobility metrics provide insight into how well an organization fosters career growth opportunities, encourages talent development, and supports employee retention through internal progression.

Significance:

Promotion and internal mobility are critical indicators of how well an organization manages talent and fosters career development. When employees see that there are opportunities for advancement within the company, they are more likely to remain engaged, motivated, and committed to the organization. A high promotion rate and strong internal mobility can lead to better retention, reduce turnover costs, and create a more skilled and loyal workforce. Furthermore, internal mobility allows companies to leverage their existing talent pool, ensuring they are making the best use of employees' skills, experiences, and knowledge.

Why It's Important:

1. **Talent Retention:** Promotion and internal mobility are key to retaining employees. If employees perceive they have no growth opportunities within the organization, they may seek career advancement elsewhere.
2. **Employee Engagement and Motivation:** Employees who are promoted or have opportunities for internal movement feel recognized and valued, leading to higher engagement and job satisfaction.
3. **Cost-Effective Talent Development:** Promoting from within is typically less expensive than recruiting externally. Organizations save on recruitment costs, onboarding, and training when they promote existing employees.
4. **Organizational Knowledge Retention:** Internal mobility ensures that employees who understand the company culture, processes, and systems can continue to contribute at higher levels, reducing the risk of losing critical organizational knowledge.
5. **Diversity and Inclusion:** Promoting diversity and ensuring inclusive mobility opportunities within the organization helps foster a culture of fairness and equal opportunity, which can improve organizational culture and morale.

- Evaluates career growth opportunities within an organization.
- Formula: (Number of internal promotions / Total employees) × 100.
- Encourages employee development and reduces external hiring costs.

Conclusion

KPIs in HR analytics provide critical insights that enhance workforce management and drive business performance. By tracking and optimizing these key metrics, HR departments can create data-driven strategies to improve recruitment, engagement, retention, and overall organizational success. Future trends include AI-driven HR analytics, predictive modeling, and enhanced employee experience analytics.

CHAPTER TEN

Evaluating the Impact of Demand Forecasting on Sustainable Development Goals

Author: Dr. Shilpi Kavita, Assistant Professor at St. Xaviers College of Management and Tecnology, Patna, Bihar

Abstract:

Demand forecasting plays a crucial role in ensuring that resources are allocated efficiently across industries, businesses, and supply chains. In the context of sustainable development, accurate demand forecasting is integral to achieving the United Nations' Sustainable Development Goals (SDGs), particularly those related to responsible consumption and production, climate action, and economic growth. This study explores the impact of demand forecasting on advancing sustainable development, assessing how its application can contribute to achieving specific SDGs.

Through a combination of quantitative analysis and case studies, this research investigates how demand forecasting practices influence sustainability outcomes in various sectors, including energy, manufacturing, agriculture, and retail. Key focus areas include minimizing waste, optimizing resource utilization, reducing carbon footprints, and promoting circular economy principles. The study evaluates the role of modern forecasting techniques, such as machine learning and big data analytics, in enhancing the accuracy of demand predictions and in turn, supporting the efficient use of resources.

Findings from the study indicate that demand forecasting significantly contributes to reducing overproduction and underproduction, leading to less

resource wastage and lower environmental impacts. In sectors like agriculture and energy, accurate forecasting enables better planning of production schedules, resource allocation, and supply chain management, directly supporting SDG 12 (Responsible Consumption and Production) and SDG 13 (Climate Action). Furthermore, businesses that implement advanced demand forecasting tools are able to align their operations with sustainable practices, fostering long-term economic growth and reducing inequalities, in line with SDG 8 (Decent Work and Economic Growth) and SDG 10 (Reduced Inequalities).

However, the study also highlights challenges in integrating demand forecasting with sustainability goals, including data quality, technological infrastructure limitations, and the need for stakeholder collaboration. It underscores the importance of adopting a holistic approach that considers social, environmental, and economic factors when implementing forecasting models.

In conclusion, demand forecasting has a significant and multifaceted impact on the achievement of Sustainable Development Goals. By improving resource efficiency and reducing negative environmental impacts, it supports the transition to a more sustainable and equitable global economy. For maximum impact, businesses and policymakers must prioritize the integration of demand forecasting with sustainability strategies to achieve long-term development goals.

Introduction

Demand forecasting plays a crucial role in achieving Sustainable Development Goals (SDGs) by optimizing resource allocation, reducing waste, and enhancing economic stability. Accurate forecasting allows businesses, governments, and organizations to plan effectively, ensuring sustainable consumption and production patterns. This study explores the impact of demand forecasting on SDGs and its significance in promoting environmental, social, and economic sustainability.

Demand forecasting is a critical tool for ensuring that resources are used efficiently and sustainably, aligning with the Sustainable Development Goals (SDGs) set by the United Nations. By predicting future demand for goods and services, businesses, governments, and organizations can optimize their planning processes, minimize waste, and allocate resources effectively. In this context, demand forecasting directly contributes to SDG

12: Responsible Consumption and Production, but it also has far-reaching effects on other goals such as economic growth, environmental protection, and social equity.

Role of Demand Forecasting in SDGs

Demand forecasting plays a crucial role in advancing the Sustainable Development Goals (SDGs) by improving the efficiency and sustainability of production and consumption systems. By accurately predicting future demand for goods and services, organizations can optimize resource use, reduce waste, and minimize negative environmental impacts, all while supporting economic growth and social well-being.

Demand forecasting is a vital tool for aligning business strategies with sustainability goals, contributing to SDG 12: Responsible Consumption and Production and impacting other SDGs such as SDG 13: Climate Action, SDG 8: Decent Work and Economic Growth, and SDG 10: Reduced Inequalities.

1. Reducing Waste and Enhancing Resource Efficiency

One of the most significant contributions of demand forecasting to the Sustainable Development Goals (SDGs) is its ability to reduce waste and enhance resource efficiency, which directly supports SDG 12: Responsible Consumption and Production. Accurate demand forecasting allows organizations to predict and plan their production processes more effectively, ensuring that resources are used optimally, and excess goods are avoided. This not only leads to cost savings but also plays a critical role in minimizing environmental impact by reducing waste and conserving natural resources.

- Demand forecasting helps minimize overproduction and excess inventory.
- Aligns supply chain operations with sustainable resource management (SDG 12: Responsible Consumption and Production).

2. Promoting Economic Growth and Employment Stability

Demand forecasting plays a crucial role in promoting economic growth and ensuring employment stability, which are key objectives of SDG 8: Decent Work and Economic Growth. By providing businesses with the data needed to predict consumer demand and adjust production accordingly, demand forecasting helps create an efficient, resilient, and sustainable economic environment. It allows organizations to make more informed decisions regarding resource allocation, investment, and workforce planning, thereby driving both economic stability and job creation.

- Forecasting aids in business expansion and workforce planning.
- Reduces financial uncertainty and supports sustainable economic growth (SDG 8: Decent Work and Economic Growth).

3. Improving Food Security and Agricultural Sustainability

Demand forecasting is essential in improving food security and promoting agricultural sustainability, which are integral to achieving SDG 2: Zero Hunger and SDG 12: Responsible Consumption and Production. By accurately predicting demand for food products, agricultural businesses, governments, and organizations can make informed decisions regarding resource allocation, production planning, and distribution. This ultimately helps ensure a stable food supply, minimizes waste, and promotes sustainable agricultural practices that can withstand environmental challenges.

- Enables precise planning for food production and distribution.
- Reduces food waste and ensures food availability in vulnerable regions (SDG 2: Zero Hunger).

4. Enhancing Energy Efficiency and Climate Action

Demand forecasting plays a crucial role in enhancing energy efficiency and supporting climate action, which are essential components of SDG 7: Affordable and Clean Energy and SDG 13: Climate Action. By predicting future energy needs and consumption patterns, demand forecasting helps utilities, businesses, and governments make informed decisions that reduce energy waste, optimize resource usage, and minimize the environmental impact of energy production and consumption. This, in turn, supports the transition to a more sustainable and resilient energy system, contributing to global efforts in combating climate change.

- Forecasting energy demand supports the transition to renewable sources.
- Reduces energy wastage and promotes sustainable consumption (SDG 7: Affordable and Clean Energy, SDG 13: Climate Action).

5. Optimizing Healthcare and Medical Supply Chains

Demand forecasting plays a critical role in optimizing healthcare and medical supply chains, which are crucial to achieving SDG 3: Good Health and Well-Being. By predicting the demand for healthcare services, pharmaceuticals, medical equipment, and supplies, demand forecasting helps improve the efficiency, reliability, and sustainability of healthcare systems. It ensures that resources are allocated effectively, shortages are avoided, and costs are minimized, ultimately improving patient outcomes and ensuring that healthcare services are accessible to all, particularly during times of crisis like pandemics or natural disasters.

- Helps in predicting the demand for medical supplies and services.
- Enhances the efficiency of healthcare systems and ensures accessibility (SDG 3: Good Health and Well-being).

Challenges in Implementing Demand Forecasting for SDGs

While demand forecasting plays a significant role in achieving the Sustainable Development Goals (SDGs), its successful implementation faces several challenges. These challenges stem from technological, data-related, organizational, and contextual issues that make accurate and actionable forecasting complex and difficult. Understanding these challenges is essential to improving forecasting models and leveraging them for sustainable development.

1. Data Accuracy and Availability

Data accuracy and availability pose significant challenges in demand forecasting for achieving the Sustainable Development Goals (SDGs). Reliable, accurate data is essential for generating effective forecasts, as any inaccuracies or gaps can lead to poor decision-making and resource misallocation. In many regions, particularly in developing countries or rural areas, there are significant gaps in data, often due to underdeveloped data collection systems. This can hinder the ability to predict demand for essential resources like food, healthcare, and energy. Moreover, inconsistent or outdated data further complicates forecasting efforts. Errors or discrepancies in data, such as incorrect disease prevalence figures in healthcare or mismatched food security data, can distort forecasts, leading to the misallocation of resources. The absence of standardized data collection methods across regions or sectors only exacerbates these issues, making it difficult to harmonize and interpret data effectively. Additionally, outdated data, or delays in data reporting, can render forecasts obsolete, especially in fast-changing areas such as renewable energy demand or climate change mitigation efforts. Lastly, the lack of granular data at the local or community level often limits the effectiveness of forecasts, as national or regional data may not capture specific, localized demand patterns. Without accurate and up-to-date data, the implementation of demand forecasting for SDGs becomes less reliable, reducing its potential to optimize resources and achieve sustainable development outcomes.

- Incomplete or outdated data can impact forecasting reliability.
- Requires advanced data analytics and real-time tracking mechanisms.

2. Technological and Infrastructure Barriers

Technological and infrastructure barriers are significant challenges in implementing demand forecasting for the Sustainable Development Goals (SDGs). Effective forecasting relies heavily on advanced technologies such as artificial intelligence (AI), machine learning, big data analytics, and cloud computing. However, in many regions, especially in developing countries or remote areas, the technological infrastructure needed to support these systems is either lacking or underdeveloped. Many organizations, particularly those in rural or underserved regions, struggle with limited access to high-speed internet, insufficient computing resources, and a lack of advanced analytics tools. This limits their ability to collect and process large volumes of data in real time, which is crucial for accurate demand forecasting.

Furthermore, outdated or incompatible software and hardware can prevent the effective integration of new technologies that drive modern forecasting models. For instance, healthcare or agricultural systems may rely on legacy technologies that do not support the seamless collection, storage, or analysis of data needed for accurate demand projections. This technological divide can create a gap between those who can leverage advanced forecasting tools and those who cannot, exacerbating inequalities in resource distribution and SDG achievement.

In addition to technological limitations, insufficient infrastructure such as electricity supply, telecommunication networks, and data storage facilities can further hinder the ability to implement effective demand forecasting. Without reliable and scalable infrastructure, the consistent collection and processing of data becomes a challenge, leading to delays, inefficiencies, and ultimately less effective decision-making for achieving sustainable development.

These barriers make it difficult to adopt cutting-edge forecasting methods in many parts of the world, limiting the potential of demand forecasting to optimize resources, reduce waste, and meet the ambitious targets set by the SDGs. Addressing these technological and infrastructure challenges is essential to making demand forecasting a practical and impactful tool in the global effort towards sustainability.

- Developing nations face challenges in adopting AI-driven forecasting models.
- Investment in digital transformation is crucial for accurate demand prediction.

3. Regulatory and Policy Constraints

Regulatory and policy constraints present significant challenges in the effective implementation of demand forecasting for achieving the Sustainable Development Goals (SDGs). Governments and organizations across the globe often operate within complex regulatory environments that can limit the ability to collect, share, and use data for forecasting purposes. Strict data privacy laws, bureaucratic procedures, and policy restrictions may impede the flow of essential data between sectors or across borders, which is crucial for creating accurate forecasts. For instance, in sectors like healthcare, education, or energy, where cross-sector data sharing is necessary for holistic forecasting, policies that restrict data sharing or make data collection overly complicated can slow down the entire process.

In many countries, regulatory frameworks may not be updated to accommodate the rapid advances in digital technologies or the increasing need for data-driven decision-making in areas such as climate action or resource management. For example, outdated environmental regulations may fail to consider new sustainable technologies or green innovations, thereby limiting forecasting models that rely on the integration of such technologies into long-term planning. Similarly, trade policies or subsidy structures in agriculture, energy, or manufacturing may skew demand forecasts, as governments may regulate the prices or availability of resources in ways that do not reflect actual market needs or sustainable practices.

Furthermore, policy fragmentation between local, national, and international governance structures can create barriers to effective forecasting. For instance, without clear policy alignment on climate change adaptation, food security, or sustainable urban planning, different levels of government may generate conflicting or incompatible data, complicating efforts to forecast needs for essential resources accurately. Political instability or changing government priorities can also disrupt long-term forecasting efforts, especially when shifts in policies affect the consistency and continuity of data collection or resource allocation.

To overcome these barriers, a coordinated approach between policymakers, data scientists, and industry stakeholders is necessary to update regulations and create flexible, forward-thinking policies that facilitate data-driven decision-making. Aligning regulatory frameworks with the principles of sustainability and integrating them into forecasting processes will help overcome these constraints and drive more effective action toward achieving the SDGs.

- Inconsistent policies may hinder efficient forecasting implementation.
- Coordination between governments and businesses is necessary to integrate sustainable forecasting practices.

Future Prospects and Recommendations

The role of demand forecasting in achieving the Sustainable Development Goals (SDGs) is becoming increasingly critical as global challenges evolve. With growing technological advancements and greater emphasis on sustainability, demand forecasting holds immense potential to improve resource allocation, reduce waste, and promote economic, social, and environmental sustainability. However, to fully harness the power of forecasting, various improvements are necessary.

1. Leveraging Artificial Intelligence and Big Data

Leveraging Artificial Intelligence (AI) and Big Data for demand forecasting is a game-changer in advancing the Sustainable Development Goals (SDGs). AI, particularly through machine learning and predictive analytics, enables the analysis of vast amounts of data from diverse sources to identify patterns and trends that would otherwise go unnoticed. This capability enhances the accuracy of demand forecasts across sectors such as energy, healthcare, agriculture, and supply chains, leading to more informed decision-making. Big Data, when combined with AI, allows real-time analysis of dynamic data streams—such as weather patterns, economic shifts, and social trends—enabling faster responses to evolving needs. For instance, in agriculture, AI-driven forecasts can predict crop yields based on climate data, optimizing resource allocation and minimizing waste, while in energy, it can predict consumption patterns, ensuring efficient production and distribution. The integration of these technologies also fosters sustainability by enabling better planning, reducing overproduction, and ensuring resources are allocated where they are needed most. Ultimately, by combining AI's computational power with Big Data's vast scope, we can achieve more sustainable, efficient, and accurate demand forecasting, significantly contributing to SDGs like affordable energy (SDG 7), food security (SDG 2), and climate action (SDG 13).

- AI-driven predictive analytics can enhance forecasting accuracy.
- Integrating IoT and blockchain technologies for real-time data monitoring.

2. Collaboration Between Public and Private Sectors

Collaboration between the public and private sectors is crucial for leveraging demand forecasting to achieve the Sustainable Development Goals (SDGs). Both sectors bring unique strengths to the table: the public sector often has access to large-scale data, regulatory frameworks, and broad policy-making powers, while the private sector has innovation, technological expertise, and the ability to scale solutions efficiently. When these strengths are combined, they can create synergies that improve demand forecasting and lead to more sustainable, impactful outcomes.

For example, in the energy sector, governments can provide regulatory support for renewable energy integration, while private companies can bring cutting-edge technologies, like smart grids and energy storage solutions, to the table. This collaboration enables more accurate demand forecasts, ensuring that energy is produced and distributed efficiently, supporting SDG 7 (Affordable and Clean Energy). Similarly, in healthcare, public sector agencies can ensure that essential health data is collected and shared, while private companies can leverage AI and data analytics to improve medical supply chain forecasting, which is critical for SDG 3 (Good Health and Well-being).

This partnership is also vital in addressing global issues like climate change and food security, where large-scale data and advanced forecasting tools are needed to predict resource shortages, plan infrastructure, and mitigate risks. The public sector can provide policy support and data governance, while the private sector can develop innovative tools and solutions to improve forecasting accuracy and optimize resource allocation. By working together, the public and private sectors can overcome challenges, improve efficiency, and accelerate progress toward achieving the SDGs.

- Encouraging partnerships for knowledge sharing and policy alignment.
- Government incentives for businesses adopting sustainable forecasting models.

3. Capacity Building and Awareness Programs

Capacity building and awareness programs are essential to ensuring the successful implementation of demand forecasting for achieving the Sustainable Development Goals (SDGs). These programs play a pivotal role in equipping individuals, communities, organizations, and governments with the necessary skills, knowledge, and tools to understand and utilize demand forecasting effectively. By fostering expertise in key sectors such as data analytics, technology integration, and sustainable practices, these initiatives can significantly enhance decision-making processes and resource management.

For example, in developing regions, where access to advanced technology and data analytics tools may be limited, training programs can empower local communities to utilize simple forecasting methods. This can help optimize local resources, improve agricultural practices, manage water resources more efficiently, and reduce waste, contributing directly to SDG 2 (Zero Hunger) and SDG 6 (Clean Water and Sanitation). Additionally, awareness campaigns targeting sustainable practices can promote better demand management, guiding communities on how to use resources more efficiently while minimizing environmental impact.

Governments and organizations can partner with universities, NGOs, and private companies to develop tailored capacity-building programs that are context-specific, addressing the unique challenges of each region. These programs can also focus on digital literacy, enabling people to use forecasting tools and artificial intelligence (AI) models, which can be particularly beneficial for achieving SDG 9 (Industry, Innovation, and Infrastructure).

Moreover, raising awareness about the importance of data-driven decision-making can drive broader adoption of demand forecasting across sectors, from healthcare to energy management. By building local capacities and promoting awareness, these programs ensure that all stakeholders—from policymakers to local farmers—can make informed decisions that contribute to more sustainable, equitable, and efficient resource allocation in line with the SDGs.

- Training stakeholders on the importance of demand forecasting in sustainability.
- Promoting research and innovation in forecasting techniques.

Conclusion

Demand forecasting is a powerful tool in achieving Sustainable Development Goals by promoting efficient resource use, economic stability, and environmental sustainability. While challenges exist, advancements in technology and policy reforms can enhance the effectiveness of demand forecasting in driving sustainable development. Integrating forecasting models with sustainability strategies will contribute to a more resilient and equitable global economy.

CHAPTER ELEVEN

HRM : Talent Acquisition and Retention in the Modern Workforce

Author: Miss. Anushka, Research Scholar at Sam Higginbottom University of Agriculture Technology & Sciences, Prayagraj, U.P

Co-Author: Dr. Sneh P. Daniel (Associate Professor, Sam Higginbottom University of Agriculture Technology & Sciences)

Abstract:

In today's rapidly evolving business environment, talent acquisition and retention have become critical factors for organizational success. Human Resource Management (HRM) plays a pivotal role in not only attracting top talent but also ensuring that employees remain engaged and committed to the organization. This study explores the strategies and challenges related to talent acquisition and retention in the modern workforce, focusing on how HRM practices can effectively address the changing expectations of employees and the competitive landscape for talent.

The research examines the impact of various factors on talent acquisition, including employer branding, recruitment technology, diversity and inclusion initiatives, and the role of social media in attracting candidates. Additionally, it investigates the growing importance of employee retention strategies, particularly in light of increasing turnover rates and the shifting preferences of younger generations, such as millennials and Gen Z. Key retention strategies explored include career development opportunities, work-life balance, compensation and benefits, organizational culture, and leadership quality.

The findings suggest that organizations that adopt a holistic and personalized approach to talent acquisition and retention are better equipped

to build a skilled and committed workforce. Advanced recruitment technologies, such as AI-driven applicant tracking systems and data analytics, are enhancing hiring processes, enabling HR professionals to identify the best-fit candidates efficiently. On the retention front, fostering a positive work culture, offering continuous learning opportunities, and providing flexible working arrangements are identified as crucial factors in reducing turnover and boosting employee satisfaction.

However, the study also highlights challenges, such as the pressure to meet recruitment demands, the increasing need for upskilling programs, and the complexities of managing remote or hybrid workforces. As the global talent pool becomes more diverse, organizations must adapt their HRM strategies to stay competitive while meeting the evolving expectations of employees.

In conclusion, talent acquisition and retention are indispensable to organizational success in the modern workforce. HRM practices that focus on attracting diverse talent and fostering a supportive, engaging work environment are essential for maintaining a motivated, high-performing workforce. As the labor market continues to evolve, organizations must remain agile and forward-thinking to navigate the challenges and opportunities presented by changing talent dynamics.

Introduction

This chapter provides an in-depth exploration of talent acquisition and retention strategies in the modern workforce. In today's dynamic business environment, organizations face numerous challenges in attracting, hiring, and retaining top talent. These challenges are compounded by rapid technological advancements, shifting workforce expectations, and an increasingly global talent pool. The chapter examines the evolving landscape of talent acquisition and retention, highlighting innovative strategies, tools, and technologies that HR professionals are leveraging to address these challenges. Moreover, it delves into the critical role of company culture, employee experience, and workforce engagement in retention efforts.

Talent acquisition and retention are two of the most critical functions within human resource management (**HRM**) that directly impact an organization's ability to thrive in a competitive market. With businesses striving to stay ahead of the curve in an ever-changing global economy, attracting and keeping top talent has become not just a priority but a strategic necessity. As organizations face labor shortages, skill gaps, and heightened competition for talent, innovative and forward-thinking HR practices are required to ensure they can secure the right talent and keep them engaged and motivated.

This chapter outlines the significant trends, challenges, and best practices in talent acquisition and retention, helping HR professionals understand how to better navigate this complex terrain.

1. The Evolution of Talent Acquisition

Talent acquisition has undergone significant transformations over the past few decades, evolving from a reactive, administrative function to a proactive, strategic endeavor that plays a central role in business success. Historically, talent acquisition focused primarily on filling open positions, often through traditional methods like job postings in newspapers or reliance on internal referrals. However, as organizations recognized the increasing importance of human capital in driving innovation and growth, talent acquisition began to shift toward a more sophisticated, data-driven, and candidate-centric approach.

1.1 Traditional vs. Modern Talent Acquisition

Traditionally, talent acquisition was primarily about filling vacancies as quickly as possible. It often relied on reactive approaches, such as posting job advertisements and reviewing resumes. However, modern talent acquisition has become a more strategic, proactive process, aimed at building a long-term talent pipeline. Key advancements in talent acquisition include:

- **Shift from Job Boards to Digital Platforms:** In the digital age, job boards and classified ads have been supplemented, or in some cases replaced, by digital platforms such as LinkedIn, Glassdoor, Indeed, and others. These platforms offer access to a global talent pool, sophisticated search algorithms, and targeted job recommendations.
- **AI and Automation in Recruitment:** Artificial intelligence (AI) and automation have revolutionized recruitment processes by streamlining tasks such as resume screening, interview scheduling, and candidate sourcing. AI tools help recruiters quickly identify the most qualified candidates by matching job descriptions with candidate profiles, thus enhancing the efficiency and quality of hiring.
- **Video Interviews and Remote Hiring:** With the rise of remote work, video interviews have become commonplace. Technology allows for

seamless, virtual interview experiences, ensuring that geographical barriers do not hinder the hiring process. AI-powered interview platforms are also being used to analyze candidate responses, helping recruiters make data-driven hiring decisions.

1.2 Employer Branding and Candidate Experience

Employer branding plays a central role in talent acquisition. In today's highly competitive job market, companies need to build a strong employer brand that resonates with potential candidates. This involves creating a compelling narrative around the company's values, culture, and mission. A positive candidate experience also contributes to employer branding, where transparent communication, timely feedback, and a respectful interview process lead to candidates perceiving the company as a desirable place to work.

2. The Importance of Data-Driven Recruitment

Data analytics has transformed the way HR departments approach talent acquisition. By leveraging HR analytics, companies can make data-driven decisions that enhance hiring outcomes. Some important metrics include:

- **Time-to-Hire:** The amount of time it takes to fill a vacancy is a critical metric for HR departments. Using data, companies can identify inefficiencies in the recruitment process and reduce unnecessary delays.
- **Quality of Hire:** Rather than focusing on just filling positions quickly, organizations are increasingly measuring the success of new hires in terms of performance, productivity, and cultural fit.
- **Cost-per-Hire:** Analytics help HR departments manage recruitment budgets by tracking the cost associated with sourcing candidates, advertising, and hiring. This metric is crucial for optimizing the recruitment strategy and ensuring that companies get a good return on investment (ROI).

3. The Challenge of Talent Retention

Talent retention is one of the most significant challenges faced by organizations in today's competitive workforce environment. As businesses strive to attract the best talent, they must also invest in strategies to retain top performers and maintain a stable, engaged workforce. While acquiring talent is essential, retaining high-performing employees is just as crucial for sustaining long-term business success and competitive advantage.

The ability to retain employees is impacted by various factors, including employee engagement, career development opportunities, organizational culture, work-life balance, and the broader socio-economic environment. Given the rising costs of employee turnover—such as recruitment expenses, training, and the loss of institutional knowledge—organizations must adopt a comprehensive and proactive approach to retention.

3.1 Factors Influencing Employee Retention

Talent retention remains one of the most significant challenges facing organizations today. High turnover rates are costly, disrupting team dynamics and productivity. Some critical factors that influence employee retention include:

- **Company Culture:** A strong, positive company culture is one of the most effective tools in retaining talent. Organizations that prioritize inclusivity, open communication, work-life balance, and employee recognition foster loyalty and job satisfaction. Employees who feel they are part of a supportive culture are more likely to remain with the organization.

- **Career Development and Growth:** Employees are more likely to stay with organizations that provide opportunities for continuous learning and professional development. Companies that offer career advancement programs, mentorship, and skills training are more successful in retaining talent, as employees see a clear path for growth within the organization.

- **Compensation and Benefits:** Competitive compensation packages are essential for attracting and retaining talent. However, it's not just about salary—benefits such as health insurance, retirement savings plans, flexible working hours, and wellness programs play a significant role in enhancing employee satisfaction and reducing turnover.

- **Work-Life Balance:** Employees increasingly value flexibility in their work arrangements. Organizations that offer flexible hours, remote working options, and support for personal well-being tend to retain employees longer. During the pandemic, many companies realized the importance of flexible work policies and have maintained or expanded them even as normalcy returns.

3.2 The Role of Employee Engagement in Retention

Employee engagement is closely linked to retention. Engaged employees are more productive, loyal, and committed to their employer. Key drivers of engagement include:

- **Recognition and Reward:** Employees who feel appreciated and recognized for their hard work are more likely to stay with an organization. Recognition programs, both formal (like awards and bonuses) and informal (such as verbal praise), can increase morale and motivation.
- **Regular Feedback and Communication:** Continuous feedback mechanisms, such as regular one-on-one meetings, surveys, and performance reviews, foster an open dialogue between employees and managers. Employees who feel heard and valued are more likely to stay engaged and committed to the company.
- **Empowerment and Autonomy:** Giving employees the freedom to make decisions and contribute to company goals increases their sense of ownership and satisfaction. This can be achieved through delegation of responsibility, involvement in strategic discussions, and opportunities for leadership development.

4. Best Practices for Talent Acquisition and Retention

As the modern workforce continues to evolve, organizations must adopt effective strategies to attract, acquire, and retain top talent. Implementing best practices in both talent acquisition and retention is crucial to building a competitive workforce and achieving long-term organizational success. Below are several best practices that organizations can adopt to optimize their talent acquisition and retention strategies.

- **4.1 Building an Inclusive and Diverse Workforce** Inclusion and diversity are essential for attracting and retaining talent. Organizations that embrace diversity in all its forms—gender, race, age, and background—tend to perform better and experience higher employee satisfaction. HR departments should focus on building diverse teams through inclusive recruitment practices and promoting a culture of equity and belonging.
- **4.2 Onboarding and Socialization** The onboarding process is crucial for retention. A well-structured onboarding program that familiarizes new hires with the company culture, expectations, and values enhances their

experience and helps them integrate more smoothly into their roles. A positive initial experience can significantly increase the likelihood that employees will stay long term.

- **4.3 Employee Well-Being Programs** Comprehensive employee well-being programs that focus on physical, emotional, and financial well-being contribute to higher retention rates. This includes offering mental health support, wellness programs, flexible schedules, and ensuring a healthy work environment.

5. The Future of Talent Acquisition and Retention

As the workforce continues to evolve, HR professionals must adapt to emerging trends. The growing reliance on artificial intelligence and machine learning for recruitment will continue to shape talent acquisition, while employee well-being and flexibility will remain central to retention strategies. Additionally, as hybrid work models become more mainstream, organizations will need to rethink how they engage and retain remote employees.

Conclusion

Talent acquisition and retention are interconnected and vital for the long-term success of organizations. To stay competitive in a fast-paced and evolving job market, companies must continuously innovate their recruitment strategies and focus on creating a positive, supportive, and engaging work environment. By leveraging data, embracing diversity, and prioritizing employee engagement, HR professionals can ensure they attract and retain the talent necessary for organizational growth and success.

CHAPTER TWELVE

Transactional Efficiency of Transformational Empathy : Redefing HR Practices in the digital Age

Author: Poodari Rohith Goud, Research Scholar at Aligarh Muslim University Aligarh , U.P

Abstract:

In the digital age, the role of Human Resource (HR) management is evolving to meet the demands of a rapidly changing workplace landscape. As technology advances, organizations are increasingly relying on digital tools to enhance transactional HR practices, while simultaneously seeking more empathetic, transformational approaches to leadership and employee engagement. This study explores the concept of transformational empathy—a blend of empathetic leadership and innovative digital practices—and its impact on the transactional efficiency of HR processes. The research delves into how transformational empathy can redefine HR practices, fostering a more holistic, human-centered approach to organizational development and employee experience.

The study investigates the integration of empathy-driven leadership with digital technologies, such as artificial intelligence (AI), machine learning, and data analytics, which are traditionally focused on transactional efficiency in HR activities like recruitment, performance management, and employee retention. By combining these two seemingly divergent elements, transformational empathy aims to humanize digital HR practices, aligning them with the emotional and psychological needs of employees while maintaining operational efficiency. Key areas of focus include recruitment and onboarding, performance feedback, employee well-being programs, and leadership development.

The findings indicate that integrating empathy into HR practices significantly improves employee engagement, satisfaction, and retention, despite the digitalization of traditional HR functions. While digital tools streamline administrative tasks and provide data-driven insights, the incorporation of empathy fosters a more connected and supportive work environment, which enhances trust, communication, and collaboration across the organization. Furthermore, transformational empathy helps address challenges related to remote work, diversity and inclusion, and mental health in the workplace—issues that have gained prominence in the digital era.

However, the study also highlights challenges such as the potential for technology to depersonalize interactions, the need for HR professionals to develop new skills in both digital fluency and emotional intelligence, and the importance of ensuring that empathy does not become a superficial or tokenistic gesture.

In conclusion, the transactional efficiency of HR practices can be greatly enhanced by adopting transformational empathy, creating a balanced approach that combines the best of both technological advancements and human-centered leadership. As organizations navigate the complexities of the digital age, redefining HR practices through empathetic, transformational leadership can lead to more sustainable, productive, and positive work environments.

Introduction

In the evolving digital age, Human Resources (HR) practices are undergoing a significant transformation, shifting from traditional methods focused on transactional efficiency to a more nuanced approach that integrates transformational empathy. While technological advancements in HR solutions, such as automation, data analytics, and cloud-based platforms, streamline administrative tasks and improve operational efficiency, they also present an opportunity to redefine how HR professionals engage with employees.

Transactional efficiency, which emphasizes speed, cost-effectiveness, and standardized processes, has long been the cornerstone of HR operations. Tools like automated payroll systems, performance management software, and AI-driven recruitment platforms have revolutionized the way HR manages tasks, providing faster results and reducing human error. However, these tools often focus on the mechanics of HR work, sometimes at the expense of the more human aspects of the employee experience.

In contrast, transformational empathy in HR represents a shift toward understanding and addressing the emotional and psychological needs of employees. It goes beyond administrative tasks to create a supportive, engaging, and inclusive workplace culture. Empathy-driven HR practices include listening actively to employee concerns, recognizing individual contributions, offering personalized career development opportunities, and fostering an environment where employees feel valued and heard.

The balance between transactional efficiency and transformational empathy is critical for organizations to thrive in today's rapidly changing work environment. While technology-driven HR solutions can optimize processes and free up time for HR professionals to focus on more strategic tasks, empathy enhances employee engagement, job satisfaction, and retention. Employees are more likely to stay with companies that show genuine care for their well-being, providing a competitive advantage in talent retention. Moreover, organizations with empathetic HR practices tend to have higher levels of employee morale, productivity, and commitment.

This study explores how HR can successfully blend the efficiency of technology with the empathy-driven approach to create a more human-centered workplace. It delves into how technology can support, rather than replace, the human aspects of HR, ensuring that both efficiency and emotional intelligence coexist to shape the future of work.

The Interplay Between Transactional Efficiency and Transformational Empathy

In today's rapidly evolving workplace, the balance between transactional efficiency and transformational empathy is becoming central to reshaping Human Resources (HR) practices. Both elements are crucial to modern HR strategy, yet they represent two distinct approaches to managing and engaging employees. Understanding their interplay allows organizations to leverage the best of both worlds—optimizing operational efficiency while also nurturing employee well-being, satisfaction, and engagement.

1. Automation and HR Efficiency

Automation and HR Efficiency have become integral components of modern human resource management, significantly transforming how HR departments operate. By leveraging automation, HR teams can streamline repetitive and time-consuming tasks such as payroll processing, benefits administration, employee data management, and recruitment workflows.

This allows HR professionals to reduce manual errors, increase accuracy, and save valuable time, ultimately boosting overall efficiency. For example, automated systems can handle routine tasks like scheduling interviews, sending reminders, and processing leave requests, freeing up HR staff to focus on more strategic initiatives like employee development and engagement. Moreover, automation tools, such as AI-driven applicant tracking systems (ATS) and onboarding software, can expedite the hiring process, ensuring that qualified candidates are quickly identified and brought into the organization. While automation enhances HR efficiency by optimizing operational processes, it also enables HR teams to provide a more personalized and responsive experience for employees, enhancing the overall effectiveness of the department. Ultimately, automation not only improves HR workflows but also fosters a more agile, data-driven approach to managing human capital.

- AI-driven HR analytics streamline recruitment, onboarding, and performance management.
- Automation reduces administrative burden, allowing HR professionals to focus on strategic initiatives.

2. Human-Centered Leadership in the Digital Era

Human-Centered Leadership in the Digital Era emphasizes the importance of maintaining a focus on people and their well-being, even as technology reshapes the workplace. In an increasingly digital world, leadership is not just about achieving operational goals or utilizing advanced technologies; it's about understanding and addressing the emotional, social, and psychological needs of employees. While digital tools and automation can drive efficiency and innovation, human-centered leadership ensures that technology is used to empower employees rather than replace or isolate them.

In the digital era, leaders must balance technological advancement with a strong emphasis on empathy, communication, and employee development. This type of leadership promotes a culture of trust, where employees feel valued, understood, and supported. For example, digital communication platforms may be used to enhance team collaboration, but they must be used thoughtfully to foster genuine connections among remote workers. Leaders must also be attuned to the unique challenges that come with digital work environments, such as feelings of isolation or burnout, and take proactive steps to address them.

Human-centered leadership involves active listening, recognizing employee contributions, and providing personalized career growth opportunities. It acknowledges that while technology can optimize processes, the human element—emotional intelligence, creativity, and collaboration—is irreplaceable. By adopting this approach, leaders can create a workplace that not only thrives technologically but also nurtures a culture of inclusion, well-being, and continuous learning, ensuring that employees are motivated and engaged in a rapidly changing environment. Ultimately, human-centered leadership in the digital era is about leveraging technology to support, rather than replace, the human experience at work.

- Digital transformation should not eliminate personal connections; rather, it should facilitate them.
- Empathy-driven leadership fosters trust and emotional well-being among employees.

3. Employee Experience and Digital Tools

Employee Experience and Digital Tools are increasingly intertwined in today's workplace, as organizations seek to enhance engagement, satisfaction, and productivity through the use of technology. Digital tools, when implemented thoughtfully, have the potential to significantly improve various aspects of the employee journey—from recruitment and onboarding to performance management and ongoing development. However, it is crucial to recognize that the use of these tools should always center around improving the overall employee experience (EX) and not merely for the sake of digitalization.

Digital platforms such as employee self-service portals, collaboration tools, and performance management systems empower employees by providing greater autonomy and accessibility. For instance, an onboarding portal allows new hires to easily access information, complete necessary paperwork, and connect with their teams before their first day, leading to a smoother and more welcoming entry into the company. Similarly, tools for continuous feedback and performance tracking enable employees to receive regular, actionable insights into their work, fostering a culture of continuous growth and recognition.

Moreover, communication tools like instant messaging platforms, virtual meeting spaces, and social collaboration networks enable seamless connectivity, especially in remote or hybrid work environments. These tools not only improve productivity and collaboration but also help create a sense of community and belonging, which is crucial for employee satisfaction. By using digital tools to streamline administrative tasks, HR teams can focus more on engaging with employees on a personal level, ensuring that their needs are met and their voices are heard.

However, for digital tools to truly enhance the employee experience, they must be intuitive, user-friendly, and designed with empathy. Employees should feel that the technology they use supports their work, reduces friction, and helps them achieve both personal and professional goals. When employees perceive digital tools as empowering, rather than burdensome, they are more likely to feel motivated and engaged in their work. Thus, HR departments must focus on selecting and implementing digital solutions that balance efficiency with a focus on human connection, ultimately creating a positive and fulfilling employee experience.

- Personalized HR tech solutions enhance employee engagement.
- Chatbots, virtual assistants, and AI-based learning platforms must be integrated with human oversight to maintain empathy in interactions.

Challenges in Balancing Efficiency and Empathy

Challenges in Balancing Efficiency and Empathy in the workplace are increasingly prominent as organizations adopt digital tools and automation to streamline processes. While technology can significantly improve operational efficiency, it can also present challenges in maintaining genuine human connection and empathy within the organization. Striking the right balance between these two forces is essential to ensure a productive and positive work environment, yet several obstacles exist in achieving this equilibrium.

1. Over-Reliance on Technology

Over-Reliance on Technology in the workplace is a growing concern, particularly as organizations continue to adopt more advanced digital tools and automation systems to streamline operations and improve efficiency. While technology can greatly enhance productivity and reduce manual workloads, an over-reliance on these tools can have unintended consequences that undermine the human aspect of work, which is essential for a thriving organizational culture.

One of the primary risks of over-relying on technology is the dehumanization of the workplace. When processes such as recruitment, performance management, and communication are heavily automated, employees may feel like they are interacting with machines rather than people. For example, automated applicant tracking systems or chatbots used for HR inquiries can create a disconnect between employees and the organization's human resources team. This lack of personal touch can lead to employees feeling disengaged, undervalued, or even alienated, as they may believe that their needs and concerns are not being truly understood or addressed.

Another challenge is the reduction in meaningful human interactions. In remote or hybrid work environments, where digital tools are essential for communication and collaboration, there is a risk that employees will miss out on face-to-face interactions with their colleagues and leaders. While technology can facilitate communication through video calls and messaging platforms, these tools often lack the emotional depth and nuance of in-person conversations. Without the ability to pick up on non-verbal cues, such as body language or tone, empathy and emotional connection can be diminished, potentially leading to misunderstandings or a lack of emotional support.

Additionally, over-reliance on technology can lead to technological burnout. As employees are bombarded with constant notifications, emails, and digital meetings, they may experience stress and fatigue from being always "on" in the digital space. The need to constantly adapt to new tools and systems can also create a sense of overwhelm, especially for those who may not be as comfortable with technology. This can lead to decreased productivity, burnout, and disengagement, which ultimately impacts both individual and organizational performance.

Lastly, an over-reliance on technology can stifle creativity and critical thinking. When employees are too focused on following automated processes or using standardized tools, they may have fewer opportunities to think outside the box or engage in creative problem-solving. This can limit innovation and reduce the agility of the organization, which is especially important in a rapidly changing business environment.

In order to avoid these pitfalls, organizations should aim for a balanced approach that integrates technology in a way that supports human interactions rather than replacing them. It's important to ensure that technology is used to enhance, not replace, empathy and human connection. Leaders should make efforts to engage with their employees personally, foster open communication, and ensure that technology does not overshadow the importance of building strong interpersonal relationships within the workplace. Additionally, regular training and support for employees in using technology can help reduce stress and make digital tools more accessible and beneficial.

- Automated HR systems may lead to impersonal decision-making.
- Lack of face-to-face interactions can reduce employee morale.

2. Data Privacy and Ethical Considerations

Data Privacy and Ethical Considerations are critical challenges in the age of digital transformation, especially as organizations increasingly rely on technology to manage sensitive employee and organizational data. With the rise of digital tools, automation, and data-driven decision-making, there is an increasing concern about how personal and sensitive information is handled, stored, and shared. Failure to address these concerns properly can lead to legal, financial, and reputational risks, as well as a breakdown in employee trust.

One of the most pressing issues is the protection of personal data. In many organizations, digital tools collect vast amounts of employee data—ranging from performance metrics and work patterns to personal information such as health data or social security numbers. Ensuring this data is stored securely and used responsibly is crucial for compliance with laws and regulations like the General Data Protection Regulation (GDPR) in Europe or data protection laws in other regions. Mishandling or exposing personal data can lead to data breaches, which not only have legal consequences but can also harm employees by compromising their privacy.

Ethical considerations come into play when discussing how organizations use the data they collect. For example, when using AI-driven recruitment tools or performance evaluation systems, the algorithms that process this data must be transparent and free from bias. If data is used to make decisions about hiring, promotions, or compensation, it is essential that these decisions are based on fair and ethical practices. Without proper oversight, there is a risk that biased algorithms could inadvertently disadvantage certain groups of employees, perpetuating inequality or discrimination in the workplace.

Another concern is the surveillance of employees. Digital tools that track employee performance, attendance, or activity levels can create a sense of constant monitoring, which may negatively affect employee morale and trust. While it's important to measure productivity, intrusive surveillance can lead to a sense of violation of privacy and a decline in employee well-being. Striking the right balance between tracking performance and respecting privacy is an ongoing challenge for HR leaders and organizations as they incorporate more digital tools.

Moreover, the ethical use of AI and machine learning algorithms in HR processes such as recruitment, promotions, and performance reviews must be carefully scrutinized. The challenge is to ensure that these algorithms do not unintentionally perpetuate biases or inequalities. If, for instance, a recruitment tool is trained on historical hiring data that reflects gender or racial biases, the algorithm may inadvertently replicate these biases, leading to unfair hiring practices. It is vital that organizations regularly audit AI systems and other automated tools to ensure they remain ethical and free from discrimination.

Employee consent is another ethical consideration when it comes to data collection and usage. Organizations must ensure that employees are fully aware of what data is being collected, how it will be used, and how it will be protected. Transparent communication is necessary to build trust with employees and ensure that they are comfortable with the data practices of the organization. Moreover, employees should have the right to opt-out or request that certain data not be collected or used, whenever possible.

Lastly, data retention policies must be carefully considered. Data should only be stored for as long as it is needed to serve its intended purpose, and organizations must ensure that data deletion protocols are in place once the data is no longer necessary. Unnecessarily retaining data can expose organizations to security risks, as well as ethical concerns about the misuse or mishandling of sensitive information.

- Employee monitoring tools must be implemented with transparency.
- Ethical AI usage ensures fair treatment and unbiased HR decisions.

3. Workforce Adaptation to Digital HR

Workforce Adaptation to Digital HR presents both opportunities and challenges as organizations embrace digital tools and technology to enhance human resource management. While digital HR solutions can improve efficiency, streamline processes, and provide valuable data insights, the transition from traditional HR practices to a more tech-driven approach requires employees to adapt to new systems, workflows, and mindsets. The success of this transformation largely depends on how well the workforce can adjust to these changes, and how well organizations support employees through the process.

One of the primary challenges in workforce adaptation to digital HR is the digital literacy gap. Not all employees possess the same level of comfort or proficiency with technology. Older employees or those who have limited experience with digital tools may find it difficult to navigate new HR systems, such as self-service portals, learning management systems, or automated performance evaluation platforms. In some cases, this can lead to frustration, disengagement, and reluctance to adopt new technologies, particularly if they feel overwhelmed by the changes or lack adequate training.

Another challenge is the cultural shift required when moving from traditional HR practices to a more digital-first approach. Many employees are accustomed to face-to-face interactions with HR representatives, whether for payroll issues, benefits inquiries, or career development discussions. Digital tools, such as automated chatbots, virtual meetings, and HR management platforms, may replace these personal interactions, which can impact the employee experience. This shift can create a sense of detachment or lack of personal connection, as employees might feel like they are dealing with a machine rather than a human being who understands their individual needs.

Furthermore, resistance to change is a common issue in workforce adaptation. People are naturally resistant to change, especially when it involves new technologies that may disrupt their established routines. Some employees might view digital HR systems as impersonal or fear that automation will replace their roles. They may also feel anxious about the accuracy of automated decisions, such as performance evaluations driven by algorithms. Overcoming this resistance requires strong leadership, clear communication, and efforts to make employees feel confident in the new systems.

Additionally, the transition to digital HR requires effective training and support. Employees need to be trained not only on how to use the new digital tools but also on how these tools can benefit them. Without proper training, employees may struggle to use the systems efficiently or fail to understand their full potential, leading to frustration and decreased productivity. Continuous support, such as help desks or user-friendly guides, is essential to help employees navigate new technologies and troubleshoot problems as they arise.

The shift to digital HR also requires a change in leadership styles. Managers need to adjust their approach to employee engagement and performance management in a digital-first world. This could involve adopting new methods for providing feedback, conducting virtual one-on-one meetings, and ensuring that employees feel connected and valued despite the physical or technological distance. Effective leadership during this transition is crucial in creating a positive experience for employees and ensuring that digital tools are seen as enablers rather than obstacles.

Finally, the integration of data analytics in digital HR tools can sometimes be intimidating for employees. HR platforms that collect, analyze, and report on employee data—such as performance metrics, attendance, and engagement levels—can feel invasive or overwhelming for employees who are not used to being monitored or assessed through data-driven means. It's important for organizations to ensure that employees understand how their data is being used, and that it is being employed to support their growth, rather than merely to track their performance.

- Resistance to digital transformation can hinder adoption.
- Upskilling programs are essential to help HR teams integrate technology with empathy-driven approaches.

Future Prospects and Recommendations

The future of workforce adaptation to digital HR is promising, driven by advancements in technology, evolving employee expectations, and the increasing need for efficiency and agility in human resource management. As organizations continue to integrate more sophisticated digital tools and data-driven approaches into their HR practices, the impact on the employee experience, organizational culture, and HR processes will be profound. However, to harness the full potential of digital HR while addressing challenges, organizations must adopt strategic initiatives that foster smooth transitions, enhance employee engagement, and ensure sustainability.

1. AI-Augmented Empathy

AI-Augmented Empathy is an emerging concept in the field of Human Resources (HR) and organizational management that aims to combine the power of artificial intelligence (AI) with human-centered, empathetic approaches. While AI excels in processing vast amounts of data, identifying patterns, and automating tasks, AI-Augmented Empathy seeks to leverage these capabilities to enhance, rather than replace, human interaction. By using AI to support and enrich the emotional and interpersonal aspects of work, organizations can improve employee engagement, satisfaction, and overall workplace culture.

In traditional HR, empathy often plays a critical role in fostering relationships, understanding employee needs, and resolving issues. However, with AI-Augmented Empathy, technology can play a supportive role in these processes, enabling HR professionals to provide personalized and timely support at scale.

- AI-driven sentiment analysis can help HR gauge employee emotions and respond proactively.
- HR chatbots should incorporate emotional intelligence to improve employee interactions.

2. Training HR Professionals in Digital Empathy

Training HR Professionals in Digital Empathy is a crucial step in adapting HR practices to the evolving digital workplace. As organizations embrace digital tools and artificial intelligence (AI) to manage human resources, it is essential that HR professionals maintain their ability to empathize and connect with employees on a human level. Digital empathy is about fostering emotional intelligence in the digital realm, where technology mediates much of the employee experience. HR professionals need to be equipped with the skills to integrate both human and digital elements to enhance employee engagement, well-being, and organizational culture.

- Empathy training combined with technological skills will prepare HR teams for the future workplace.
- Organizations should invest in leadership development programs focusing on emotional intelligence.

3. Hybrid HR Models

Hybrid HR Models represent a transformative approach to Human Resources (HR) that blends both traditional and digital strategies to create a flexible, efficient, and employee-centered HR function. As organizations adapt to changing work environments, hybrid models are emerging as a solution that integrates the best aspects of in-person and remote work, along with the use of technology, to meet the evolving needs of the workforce. This model is particularly important as businesses embrace flexible working arrangements, digital transformation, and the integration of advanced HR technologies.

- Combining digital efficiency with human interactions ensures a balanced HR ecosystem.
- Hybrid work policies should maintain flexibility while fostering a sense of belonging.

Conclusion

HR practices in the digital age must go beyond automation and efficiency by integrating transformational empathy. Organizations that balance digital HR tools with emotional intelligence will foster a more inclusive, engaged, and productive workforce. Future HR strategies should focus on augmenting technological advancements with human-centric approaches to redefine workplace culture for the better.

CHAPTER THIRTEEN

Strategic Human Resource Management in a Changing World

Author: Dr. Luxmi Sharma, Assistant Professor at BMU Rohtak, Haryana

Abstract:

Strategic Human Resource Management (SHRM) has become a critical driver of organizational success in today's rapidly changing business environment. With globalization, technological advancements, demographic shifts, and evolving employee expectations, organizations must adapt their HR strategies to maintain competitiveness and foster innovation. This study explores the evolving role of SHRM in a dynamic world, examining how strategic HR practices can align with broader organizational goals while addressing the complex challenges of the modern workplace.

The research focuses on key components of SHRM, including talent acquisition, employee development, performance management, leadership, and organizational culture, while highlighting the influence of external factors such as economic volatility, technological disruptions, and changing labor market trends. It investigates how HR leaders are shifting from traditional operational roles to more strategic positions, working closely with executives to shape business strategies that promote agility, resilience, and long-term growth.

Findings from the study indicate that organizations that adopt a proactive, forward-thinking approach to SHRM are better positioned to navigate the complexities of the changing world. These organizations embrace technology, data analytics, and automation to optimize HR processes and improve decision-making, while also prioritizing employee engagement, diversity and inclusion, and work-life balance to attract and retain top talent. Moreover, the integration of SHRM with corporate social responsibility (CSR) and sustainability initiatives is increasingly seen as essential for aligning organizational values with societal expectations.

However, the study also identifies several challenges, including resistance to change, skill gaps in the HR function, and the difficulty of balancing short-term business objectives with long-term talent management goals. The research underscores the importance of continuous learning, adaptability, and collaboration within the HR function to meet the evolving demands of the workforce and drive organizational performance.

In conclusion, SHRM plays a pivotal role in helping organizations navigate the challenges of a changing world. By aligning HR strategies with business goals, embracing technological innovations, and fostering a supportive and inclusive work environment, organizations can not only survive but thrive in a competitive and fast-paced global landscape. The study emphasizes the need for HR professionals to evolve their roles to become strategic partners in shaping the future of work.

1. Introduction

The 21st-century business landscape is characterized by constant change—driven by globalization, technological advancements, shifting workforce demographics, and evolving employee expectations. In this dynamic environment, Strategic Human Resource Management (SHRM) has moved beyond administrative tasks to become a central pillar of organizational success. The transformation from traditional HR to strategic HR reflects the increasing need for organizations to align human capital with long-term goals, navigate disruption, and build agile, future-ready workforces.

This chapter explores the evolving role of SHRM in a rapidly changing world. It highlights key trends, strategic priorities, and actionable frameworks for integrating HR practices with broader organizational strategies.

2. The Evolution of Strategic Human Resource Management

The Evolution of Strategic Human Resource Management (SHRM) represents a shift from traditional, transactional HR practices to a more proactive, value-driven approach where human resources play a central role in achieving an organization's long-term goals. Over the past few decades, the role of HR has undergone significant transformation, driven by changes in technology, organizational needs, and a deeper understanding of the strategic impact of human capital.

2.1 From Personnel Management to Strategic Partner

The evolution of Human Resource Management (HRM) has been marked by a fundamental shift from traditional personnel management to becoming a strategic partner in organizations. This transformation reflects a broader change in how businesses view their workforce—from being just a cost to being a critical driver of competitive advantage, innovation, and organizational success.

Historically, HR was viewed as a support function—managing recruitment, payroll, and compliance. Over the past few decades, however, HR has become increasingly strategic, focusing on workforce planning, leadership development, and organizational change.

2.2 Key Characteristics of SHRM

Strategic Human Resource Management (SHRM) represents a shift in how organizations view their workforce, with HR being positioned as a critical driver of business strategy rather than just an administrative function. SHRM focuses on aligning HR practices with the organization's long-term goals and ensuring that human capital contributes effectively to organizational success.

Strategic HRM is characterized by:

Strategic Human Resource Management (SHRM) is characterized by a comprehensive and forward-thinking approach that aligns HR practices with the broader organizational goals. Unlike traditional HR, which tends to focus on administrative tasks, SHRM emphasizes a proactive, long-term strategy where HR plays a key role in shaping business outcomes. This alignment with organizational goals ensures that human capital is optimally utilized to drive success. SHRM integrates data-driven decision-making, utilizing analytics to guide recruitment, performance management, and employee engagement strategies. It places a strong focus on talent management and development, ensuring that the right talent is recruited, nurtured, and retained to meet future business needs. Additionally, SHRM fosters a positive employee experience, aiming to enhance employee engagement, well-being, and career development, which are essential for organizational success. The approach also emphasizes the development of leadership through succession planning and ensures the workforce is adaptable and prepared for change, helping the organization stay agile in a dynamic business environment. Furthermore, SHRM promotes workforce diversity and inclusion, recognizing that a diverse workforce drives innovation and enhances performance. In essence, SHRM is characterized by its focus on long-term organizational success, its integration with business strategy, and its role in creating a workforce that is both skilled and engaged.

- Alignment of HR practices with organizational mission and vision
- Long-term planning and forecasting workforce needs
- Proactive talent management that anticipates business shifts
- Integration across departments and business functions

3. Forces Shaping the HR Landscape

The landscape of Human Resource Management (HRM) is constantly evolving, influenced by various internal and external forces. These forces shape how HR professionals approach their roles, impacting everything from talent acquisition to employee development and organizational culture.

3.1 Technological Disruption

Technological disruption is reshaping the way organizations approach HR, driving profound changes in job design, performance evaluation, learning and development, and talent management. Technologies such as automation, artificial intelligence (AI), and data analytics are revolutionizing HR practices, making them more efficient, data-driven, and personalized. As these technologies become integral to HR processes, strategic HR leaders must understand their impact and leverage them to enhance organizational effectiveness and employee experience.

3.2 Workforce Diversity and Inclusion

Workforce diversity and inclusion (D&I) have become fundamental pillars of modern organizational strategy. Today's organizations are recognizing that embracing diversity—across gender, race, age, culture, and neurodiversity—enhances creativity, improves decision-making, and strengthens organizational performance. Strategic Human Resource Management (SHRM) plays a crucial role in fostering inclusive hiring practices, reducing bias, and creating equitable workplaces where all employees feel valued, respected, and empowered.

3.3 Remote Work and Flexibility

The COVID-19 pandemic dramatically accelerated the adoption of remote and hybrid work models, compelling organizations to quickly adapt to a new way of working. What began as a temporary response to health and safety concerns has now become a fundamental shift in how businesses operate. Strategic Human Resource Management (SHRM) is tasked with redefining employee engagement, productivity, and collaboration within decentralized teams, ensuring that organizations continue to thrive in this new work environment.

3.4 Globalization

In an increasingly interconnected world, globalization has become a defining factor in the way organizations operate. As businesses expand across borders, Strategic Human Resource Management (SHRM) faces the challenge of managing a workforce that is geographically dispersed, culturally diverse, and subject to various legal and regulatory frameworks. To navigate this complexity, HR strategies must adapt to respect cultural differences, comply with local labor laws, and support global talent mobility, all while maintaining organizational coherence and alignment with the company's goals and values.

4. Strategic Priorities in SHRM

Strategic Human Resource Management (SHRM) plays a vital role in aligning HR practices with the long-term objectives of an organization. To drive sustainable growth, employee satisfaction, and competitive advantage, HR leaders must focus on several key strategic priorities. These priorities ensure that HR functions not only manage talent effectively but also contribute to the overall business strategy and success.

4.1 Talent Acquisition and Employer Branding

Talent acquisition and employer branding are two of the most critical strategic priorities in SHRM today. As organizations strive to attract top talent and maintain a competitive edge, it is essential to not only have effective recruitment strategies but also to position the organization as an employer of choice. Together, these elements play a pivotal role in shaping the workforce, enhancing the company's reputation, and fostering long-term organizational success.

4.2 Learning and Development (L&D)

Learning and Development (L&D) is a crucial strategic priority in Strategic Human Resource Management (SHRM). In an era where continuous change is the norm, organizations must invest in developing their workforce's skills to stay competitive, innovative, and adaptable. L&D is not just about improving employees' technical competencies; it is also about fostering a culture of continuous learning and professional growth.

Strategic HR leaders must ensure that L&D initiatives are aligned with the organization's broader goals, ensuring that both individual development and business objectives are met.

Continuous learning is central to agility. SHRM emphasizes:

- Microlearning and just-in-time training
- Personalized learning journeys
- Leadership development programs
- Upskilling and reskilling for future roles

4.3 Succession Planning and Leadership Pipeline

Succession planning and the development of a leadership pipeline are integral components of Strategic Human Resource Management (SHRM). Effective succession planning ensures that organizations have a clear, structured approach to identifying and preparing future leaders, enabling the seamless continuation of operations even in the face of leadership transitions. By strategically managing talent and fostering a strong leadership pipeline, organizations not only reduce the risks associated with sudden leadership vacancies but also ensure that they are building a workforce ready to meet future challenges.

4.4 Employee Engagement and Culture

Employee engagement and organizational culture are at the heart of Strategic Human Resource Management (SHRM). Engaged employees are not just more productive; they are more committed, innovative, and aligned with the organization's mission and values. By cultivating a workplace culture that prioritizes engagement, SHRM ensures that employees feel valued, connected to the organization's purpose, and empowered to contribute their best work.

4.5 Performance Management

Performance management has undergone a significant transformation in recent years, moving away from traditional, infrequent annual reviews to more dynamic, ongoing feedback systems. In Strategic Human Resource Management (SHRM), the emphasis is now on continuous feedback, real-time goal setting, and alignment between employee performance and broader business objectives. This shift not only enhances employee development but also enables organizations to remain agile and competitive in a rapidly changing business landscape.

5. Integrating HR Strategy with Business Strategy

For an organization to thrive in today's competitive and rapidly changing business environment, Strategic Human Resource Management (SHRM) must align closely with the broader business strategy. The integration of HR strategy with business strategy ensures that people, culture, and capabilities are aligned with the organization's objectives, enabling the business to achieve its goals efficiently and effectively. This connection between HR and business strategy fosters a unified approach to achieving success, making HR a true partner in driving business performance.

This integration includes:

- Conducting HR audits to assess workforce readiness
- Developing workforce scorecards and KPIs aligned with strategic goals
- Partnering HR leaders with C-suite executives to co-create growth roadmaps
- Using predictive analytics for workforce planning and risk management

6. Case Study Snapshots

The integration of Strategic Human Resource Management (SHRM) with business strategy has been successfully demonstrated in various organizations across industries. Below are a few case study snapshots that showcase how leading companies have effectively aligned their HR strategies with business goals, leading to enhanced organizational performance and employee engagement.

6.1 Google: Building a Culture of Innovation

Google, widely recognized for its leadership in technology and innovation, has adopted a unique approach to Human Resource Management (HR) that integrates deeply with its overarching business strategy. The company's People Operations team (Google's term for HR) uses data-driven HR practices, including people analytics and continuous feedback mechanisms, to create an environment that supports and encourages innovation at every level of the organization. Google's HR strategy focuses not only on attracting top talent but also on fostering a culture of continuous learning, creativity, and collaboration that drives the company's innovation agenda.

6.2 Unilever: Future of Work Program

Unilever, a global leader in consumer goods, is renowned for its innovative approach to Strategic Human Resource Management (SHRM). As part of its Future of Work program, Unilever has introduced the "Agile

Talent Ecosystem"—an initiative designed to align its workforce with the company's business strategy in the face of rapid technological change, market shifts, and evolving consumer demands. Unilever's HR strategy emphasizes flexible roles, lifelong learning, and purpose-driven work, all while embracing automation and re-skilling programs to ensure the workforce remains agile and future-ready.

6.3 Tata Consultancy Services (TCS): Global Talent Management

Tata Consultancy Services (TCS), one of the largest global IT services companies, has long been a pioneer in Strategic Human Resource Management (SHRM), leveraging digital HR platforms to manage its expansive, globally distributed workforce. With a presence in over 45 countries, TCS is tasked with optimizing the performance and development of a diverse team across different regions and cultures. To meet these challenges, TCS has embraced digital technologies, artificial intelligence (AI), and integrated learning platforms to ensure its workforce remains agile, innovative, and aligned with the company's strategic business goals.

7. Challenges in Implementing SHRM

While Strategic Human Resource Management (SHRM) has become essential for aligning human resources with organizational goals, its implementation can face several challenges. These challenges can range from organizational culture and technology limitations to changing workforce demographics and external factors.

While SHRM offers immense value, several barriers persist:

- Misalignment between HR and top leadership
- Resistance to change within organizational culture
- Skill gaps in HR teams (e.g., analytics, digital literacy)
- Difficulty measuring the ROI of HR initiatives

Strategic HR leaders must act as change agents, building internal credibility and fostering collaboration across all levels of the organization.

8. The Future of SHRM

As businesses continue to evolve in response to technological advancements, demographic shifts, and global challenges, the role of Strategic Human Resource Management (SHRM) is becoming increasingly pivotal in shaping organizational success. The future of SHRM will be driven by innovation, adaptability, and a focus on holistic workforce management.

Looking forward, the future of SHRM will likely include:

- AI-Augmented Decision-Making in recruitment, performance, and development
- Hyper-personalized Employee Experiences driven by real-time data
- Agile HR Practices that respond quickly to business and market changes
- Sustainable HRM with a focus on social responsibility and environmental impact

Organizations that invest in SHRM today will be better positioned to thrive amid future disruptions.

9. Conclusion

Strategic Human Resource Management is no longer a luxury—it is a necessity for organizations navigating uncertainty and transformation. As the external environment continues to evolve, so too must the internal capabilities of the workforce. By aligning HR practices with strategic objectives, investing in continuous development, and fostering an inclusive, adaptable culture, organizations can unlock the full potential of their people and secure long-term competitive advantage.

CHAPTER FOURTEEN

The realm of gender disparity

Author: Srishti Bathla, Manav Rachna University, Faridabad, Haryana

Abstract:

Gender disparity remains a persistent and multifaceted issue across the globe, affecting various aspects of life, including education, employment, political participation, and social dynamics. Despite significant advancements in gender equality over the past few decades, gender disparities continue to manifest in both overt and subtle forms, limiting opportunities and perpetuating inequality. This study explores the underlying causes, manifestations, and impacts of gender disparity, with a particular focus on its implications in contemporary societies.

The research examines key areas where gender disparity remains pronounced, including the gender pay gap, underrepresentation of women in leadership roles, unequal access to education, and gender-based violence. The study also highlights how societal norms, cultural practices, and institutional biases contribute to the perpetuation of these disparities. Drawing on data from global reports, case studies, and interviews, the research explores both structural and individual factors that influence gender inequality and the ongoing challenges faced by women and gender minorities.

Findings from the study suggest that while progress has been made, gender disparity remains deeply ingrained in many aspects of social, political, and economic life. Women, particularly in developing regions, continue to face significant barriers to accessing education and healthcare, achieving economic independence, and attaining leadership positions. The study also underscores the intersectionality of gender with race, class, and other social identities, which compounds the disadvantages experienced by marginalized groups.

The research emphasizes the need for comprehensive policy reforms, social awareness campaigns, and organizational initiatives to address gender disparity. Key recommendations include promoting gender-inclusive education, strengthening legal protections for gender equality, enhancing female participation in the workforce, and challenging cultural stereotypes that reinforce traditional gender roles.

In conclusion, gender disparity is a complex and persistent issue that requires a multifaceted approach to overcome. By fostering a culture of inclusivity and equity, addressing structural inequalities, and empowering women and gender minorities, societies can take meaningful steps toward achieving true gender equality. The study calls for continued advocacy, systemic change, and collective action to dismantle the barriers that sustain gender disparity and create a more just and equitable world for all.

Introduction

Gender disparity remains a pressing issue across various sectors, affecting economic opportunities, social mobility, and workplace dynamics. Despite significant progress in promoting gender equality, disparities in pay, leadership representation, and access to opportunities persist. This study examines the scope of gender disparity, its impact on professional and personal development, and strategies for fostering a more inclusive society.

Key Areas of Gender Disparity

Gender disparity remains a significant issue in various sectors, with key areas highlighting the ongoing challenges. One of the most prominent is the pay gap, where women, on average, earn less than men for performing the same work. This disparity is compounded by occupational segregation, where women are concentrated in lower-paying industries. Additionally, career advancement and leadership opportunities are limited for women, with many facing the "glass ceiling" that prevents them from reaching executive and decision-making roles. In terms of education and training, girls and women often have less access to quality education and vocational opportunities, particularly in fields like STEM, which restricts their potential career pathways. Furthermore, healthcare and reproductive rights remain a source of gender disparity, as women often face barriers to accessing quality care, including maternal health services and reproductive healthcare. Gender-based violence also continues to disproportionately affect women, with issues like domestic violence, sexual harassment, and assault being prevalent in many societies. Work-life balance is another challenge, as women are more likely to shoulder unpaid caregiving responsibilities, limiting their ability to pursue career growth. Additionally, political representation remains skewed, with women significantly underrepresented in leadership roles and political offices. Access to financial resources also presents a barrier, with women having less access to loans and capital, hindering their economic independence and entrepreneurial aspirations. Lastly, social and cultural expectations often place restrictions on women, confining them to traditional gender roles and limiting their opportunities for personal and professional development. These key areas of gender disparity illustrate the ongoing struggle for equality and highlight the need for systemic changes to bridge the gender gap across various sectors.

Workplace Inequality

Workplace inequality refers to the unequal treatment or discrimination that employees experience based on factors such as gender, race, ethnicity, age, disability, sexual orientation, or other personal characteristics. Despite advancements in diversity and inclusion, inequality remains a significant issue in many organizations, hindering employee potential and organizational success.

- Gender pay gap continues to be a significant issue across industries.
- Women and marginalized genders face barriers to leadership roles and career advancement.
- Workplace policies often fail to address gender-specific challenges such as maternity leave and work-life balance.

Education and Skill Development

Education and skill development are fundamental to personal empowerment, economic growth, and social mobility. They serve as key drivers in addressing inequality and promoting equal opportunities across diverse sectors of society. With the rapid pace of technological advancements and shifting labor market demands, continuous learning and upskilling have become increasingly important. Here's an exploration of the role of education and skill development in shaping individuals' opportunities and promoting sustainable development.

- Limited access to quality education for girls in certain regions hinders career prospects.
- Gender biases in STEM fields discourage female participation in high-growth industries.

- Disparities in vocational training and skill development programs limit women's economic empowerment.

Economic Participation and Financial Independence

Economic participation and financial independence are critical components of personal empowerment, societal well-being, and sustainable development. These concepts focus on enabling individuals, especially those from marginalized or disadvantaged groups, to actively contribute to the economy, manage their finances effectively, and achieve economic self-sufficiency. In this context, empowering individuals to participate in economic activities and attain financial independence can significantly improve quality of life, reduce poverty, and drive economic growth.

- Women often experience restricted access to financial resources, investments, and entrepreneurship opportunities.
- Unpaid labor, including caregiving and household work, disproportionately falls on women, impacting career growth.
- Gender-based discrimination in hiring and promotions affects economic independence.

Social and Cultural Barriers

Social and cultural barriers refer to the norms, values, and practices that shape behaviors and attitudes within a society, often preventing certain individuals or groups from fully participating in various aspects of life, including education, the workforce, and social engagement. These barriers are deeply embedded in social structures and can be powerful forces that hinder equality, personal development, and overall societal progress. They often manifest in various forms such as gender discrimination, racial inequality, class stratification, and cultural norms that limit individual opportunities.

- Deep-rooted cultural norms and stereotypes reinforce gender roles and limit opportunities.
- Gender-based violence and harassment create unsafe environments in workplaces and public spaces.
- Legal and policy gaps fail to provide adequate protection against gender discrimination.

Challenges in Achieving Gender Equality

Gender equality, which ensures that individuals of all genders have equal rights, responsibilities, and opportunities, remains a significant global challenge. Despite progress in some areas, gender disparities persist across various sectors, including education, employment, healthcare, and political representation. These challenges are deeply rooted in social, cultural, economic, and political structures, making them difficult to overcome. Addressing gender inequality requires a multifaceted approach that tackles both overt and covert barriers to gender equality.

Institutional Barriers

Institutional barriers refer to the structural obstacles embedded within systems, organizations, and societal institutions that impede equal opportunities for individuals based on gender, race, class, or other factors. These barriers are often systemic and can be deeply ingrained within the policies, practices, and culture of institutions, making them difficult to overcome. Institutional barriers create inequities in various sectors, including education, the workplace, healthcare, and political representation. Tackling these barriers requires reforms at both the policy and organizational levels to ensure equal access and opportunities for all individuals.

- Lack of gender-sensitive policies in workplaces and government institutions.
- Insufficient enforcement of laws promoting gender equality.

Bias and Stereotypes

Bias and stereotypes are pervasive and deeply ingrained cognitive processes that shape how we perceive and interact with others. These mental shortcuts, often based on incomplete or oversimplified information, can influence behavior, decision-making, and relationships in both subtle and overt ways. When it comes to gender, race, class, or other identity factors, biases and stereotypes can lead to unfair treatment, discrimination, and inequality in various aspects of life, including education, employment, healthcare, and social interactions.

- Societal expectations continue to limit women's participation in leadership and decision-making roles.

- Media representation often reinforces traditional gender roles rather than challenging them.

Economic Disparities

Economic disparities refer to the unequal distribution of wealth, income, and opportunities among different groups in society. These disparities often arise from a combination of historical, structural, and systemic factors, including social class, gender, race, education, and geographic location. Economic inequality can have profound effects on individuals' lives, limiting access to resources, opportunities, and social mobility. It can perpetuate cycles of poverty, reduce quality of life, and deepen social divisions. Addressing these disparities is critical for fostering a more just and equitable society.

- Limited access to funding and resources for women entrepreneurs.
- Wage disparities persist even in progressive economies.

Strategies for Bridging Gender Disparity

Addressing gender disparity requires a concerted effort from all sectors of society, including governments, businesses, educational institutions, and individuals. Bridging gender gaps is essential for fostering a fairer, more inclusive world, where all individuals have equal access to opportunities, regardless of their gender.

Policy Reforms and Legal Protections

Achieving gender equality requires the implementation of effective policies and legal frameworks that protect and promote the rights of all individuals, regardless of gender. These reforms not only aim to eliminate barriers and discriminatory practices but also create an environment where equal opportunities and protections are guaranteed. Below are some key areas where policy reforms and legal protections are crucial in bridging gender disparity.

- Strengthening laws to prevent workplace discrimination and harassment.
- Implementing equal pay policies and enforcing transparency in wage structures.

Education and Awareness Programs

Education and awareness programs play a crucial role in addressing gender disparities by challenging stereotypes, changing attitudes, and providing individuals with the knowledge and tools needed to promote gender equality. These programs are instrumental in shifting societal norms, empowering individuals, and creating long-term cultural change. Here's a look at key strategies for effective education and awareness programs aimed at bridging gender disparities.

- Encouraging gender-neutral education and inclusive skill development programs.
- Promoting STEM education for girls and women to enhance career opportunities.

Corporate and Organizational Initiatives

Corporations and organizations have a significant role to play in reducing gender disparities. By implementing policies and practices that promote gender equality, they not only contribute to a fairer society but also enhance their own productivity and sustainability. Below are key initiatives that organizations can adopt to bridge gender gaps and create more inclusive workplaces.

- Introducing mentorship and leadership development programs for women.
- Ensuring gender-inclusive hiring practices and equal opportunities for career growth.

Community and Cultural Change

Achieving gender equality extends beyond the workplace and institutional policies—it requires deep cultural and community transformation. Societal norms, values, and behaviors often play a significant role in perpetuating gender disparities. Addressing these underlying cultural issues is key to creating lasting change. Below are some effective strategies for fostering community and cultural change that bridges gender disparities.

- Challenging societal norms that limit gender equality through advocacy and media representation.
- Encouraging men to be allies in gender equality movements.

Conclusion

Addressing gender disparity requires a multifaceted approach involving policy changes, corporate initiatives, and societal transformation. By actively promoting gender-inclusive practices and challenging stereotypes, societies can create equal opportunities for all individuals, regardless of gender. Sustainable progress depends on collective efforts from governments, organizations, and communities to dismantle barriers and foster a more equitable future.

CHAPTER FIFTEEN

Training Needs and References for Professors in Higher Education in Bihar State

Author: Santosh Kumar Yadav, Magadh University, Bodh-Gaya, Bihar

Abstract:

The quality of higher education in Bihar, like many regions, is deeply influenced by the effectiveness of its teaching faculty. Professors in Bihar's higher education institutions face unique challenges in an ever-evolving academic landscape, and their ability to adapt to modern teaching methodologies, research practices, and technological advancements is crucial for institutional success. This study explores the training needs of professors in Bihar, emphasizing the importance of continuous professional development in enhancing their teaching, research, and administrative capacities.

The research identifies several key areas where professors in Bihar require targeted training. These include pedagogical innovation, research methodology, digital literacy, leadership development, and inclusive teaching strategies. The study highlights the need for faculty to adopt modern, student-centered teaching techniques that integrate technology and digital tools, ensuring they remain relevant in a rapidly digitizing academic environment. Additionally, professors require skills in advanced research methods, data analysis, and academic publishing to contribute meaningfully to the scholarly community.

The study also explores the challenges that prevent effective faculty development, such as limited financial resources, resistance to change, lack of infrastructure, and time constraints. Addressing these barriers through

government grants, public-private partnerships, and online training platforms is vital to ensuring accessible professional development for professors in Bihar, especially those in rural and under-resourced institutions.

Moreover, the study references various training resources available to faculty, including government-funded programs, collaborative initiatives with national and international institutions, and online platforms like SWAYAM and Coursera. By leveraging these resources, professors can engage in flexible, modular, and self-paced learning that complements their teaching and research responsibilities.

In conclusion, providing comprehensive and accessible training programs for professors in Bihar is essential for enhancing the quality of higher education in the state. By addressing the identified training needs and overcoming the challenges to professional development, Bihar can foster a more competent, engaged, and innovative academic workforce, ultimately contributing to the growth and advancement of the state's higher education sector.

Introduction

Higher education in India plays a crucial role in shaping the intellectual, economic, and social fabric of the country. Within this landscape, Bihar, a state with a rich cultural history, faces unique challenges in its higher education sector. As the demand for quality education grows, so does the need for well-trained, up-to-date professors who can engage with emerging pedagogical trends and address the diverse needs of the student population. This chapter focuses on the training needs of professors in higher education in Bihar, offering insights into their professional development requirements and highlighting the significance of continuous academic training.

Training Needs for Professors in Bihar

Professors in Bihar's higher education institutions often face the dual challenge of teaching in an evolving academic environment while adapting to the diverse socio-economic backgrounds of students. Training for professors is essential to ensure they stay abreast of the latest trends in teaching methodologies, research practices, and administrative skills.

The key training needs identified for professors in Bihar are:

Pedagogical Training The traditional lecture-based teaching methods need to be supplemented with modern, interactive, and student-centered approaches. Professors require training in innovative teaching methods such as flipped classrooms, online teaching tools, and collaborative learning.

Training in technology-based pedagogy, especially in the use of digital tools for effective teaching, is particularly vital given the growing trend of digital education in India.

Research Methodology and Publication Skills The ability to conduct and publish research is a critical skill for professors, yet many institutions in Bihar still lack comprehensive support for academic research. Training in modern research methodologies, data analysis techniques, and academic writing is essential for fostering a robust research culture. Furthermore, many professors require guidance on navigating academic publishing platforms and understanding the intricacies of peer review processes.

Professional Development and Soft Skills In addition to academic skills, professors in Bihar require training in essential soft skills like communication, time management, leadership, and conflict resolution. These skills are crucial for their role in guiding students and interacting with colleagues, administrators, and the wider academic community. Moreover, leadership training is crucial for those in senior positions, as they must manage departments, mentor junior faculty, and contribute to institutional development.

Inclusive Teaching and Diversity Awareness Bihar has a large and diverse student population, including individuals from rural, marginalized, and underrepresented communities. Professors must be trained in creating inclusive learning environments that cater to the needs of students from various backgrounds. Awareness and training on diversity, inclusion, and gender sensitivity are essential to ensure that professors can engage with students in a way that fosters respect, equity, and social harmony.

Technological Training The rapid shift towards digital learning, accelerated by the COVID-19 pandemic, has created an urgent need for professors to acquire digital literacy skills. Training in the use of online platforms, virtual classrooms, digital assessment tools, and e-resources is critical for maintaining effective teaching in a digital environment. Familiarity with learning management systems (LMS) and educational software will allow professors to streamline course delivery and better engage students.

Training Programs and Resources for Professors in Bihar

Given these identified needs, various training programs and resources are available to professors in Bihar. These initiatives include:

Government-Funded Programs The Ministry of Education and state-level government bodies often provide training programs for faculty members. Initiatives such as the **National Institutional Ranking Framework (NIRF), UGCFaculty Development Program**, and various **State Council of Higher Education** programs aim to enhance the professional capabilities of professors. These programs include workshops, seminars, and online courses designed to address the diverse training needs of higher education faculty.

Collaborations with National and International Universities Many universities and academic institutions in Bihar collaborate with national and international universities to offer training and development programs. These partnerships focus on best practices in pedagogy, research collaboration, and innovative teaching methodologies. Professors can benefit from these programs through academic exchange, online certification courses, and seminars.

Online Training Platforms In response to the need for flexible training, online platforms like **SWAYAM, Coursera, edX**, and **Udemy** have become crucial resources for professors in Bihar. These platforms offer a wide range of courses on teaching methodologies, research skills, academic leadership, and technological tools. Such platforms enable professors to engage in continuous learning without the constraints of location or time.

Workshops and Seminars by Academic Bodies Several academic bodies and professional associations, such as the **Indian Academic Research Network (IARN)** and **Association of Indian Universities (AIU)**, organize workshops and seminars for faculty development. These events allow professors to stay updated with the latest developments in their respective fields and gain hands-on training in emerging teaching methods.

Local Universities and Institutes Universities in Bihar such as Patna University, Magadh University, and Bihar Agricultural University have started their own faculty development programs. These programs are aimed at improving teaching quality and aligning with the national standards set by accreditation bodies like the National Board of Accreditation (NBA) and National Assessment and Accreditation Council (NAAC).

Challenges in Implementing Training Programs

While the availability of training resources is promising, several challenges hinder their effective implementation:

Access to Resources

Access to Resources Many professors in Bihar, particularly those in rural areas, encounter significant barriers to accessing training programs due to several factors, including limited internet connectivity, inadequate infrastructure, and geographical isolation. These challenges create an uneven playing field, where professors in remote or underserved areas have fewer opportunities for professional development compared to their urban counterparts.

Limited internet connectivity is a key issue, as many rural institutions lack reliable and high-speed internet access, which makes online learning platforms, webinars, and digital resources difficult to access. Furthermore, the absence of robust infrastructure—such as computer labs, projectors, or modern teaching aids—further hinders the delivery of both traditional and digital training programs.

Geographical isolation also plays a critical role in limiting access to training opportunities. Professors in rural or distant areas often face challenges in attending physical training sessions, workshops, and seminars held in major cities or central locations. This not only restricts access to learning but also limits networking opportunities that could contribute to academic growth.

To bridge this gap and ensure equitable access to resources, there is a need for targeted initiatives aimed at improving digital infrastructure in rural areas. Providing professors with access to affordable internet services, equipping institutions with the necessary technological tools, and offering both online and offline training options can help overcome these barriers. Additionally, mobile-based learning solutions, localized content, and virtual communities of practice can also provide flexible, scalable learning alternatives that cater to the specific needs of professors in remote locations. Addressing these challenges will promote inclusivity and ensure that all educators, regardless of their location, have equal opportunities to enhance their skills and knowledge.

Resistance to Change Traditional teaching methods are deeply entrenched in many institutions, particularly in regions like Bihar, where long-established practices often shape the academic culture. Many professors, especially those with years of experience in the classroom, may be resistant to adopting new pedagogical approaches or integrating technology into their teaching practices. This resistance can stem from various factors, such as a lack of familiarity with new technologies, skepticism about their effectiveness, or fear of disrupting established routines. Additionally, the perceived effort required to learn new methods or tools may be seen as an unnecessary burden on top of already demanding academic and administrative responsibilities.

Overcoming this resistance requires a multi-faceted approach that emphasizes the importance of continuous professional development and the tangible benefits that new teaching practices and technologies can offer. Awareness programs that highlight the positive impact of modern pedagogical techniques on student engagement, learning outcomes, and academic satisfaction can help shift mindsets. For example, showcasing success stories and case studies from other institutions where innovative methods have led to improvements in teaching and learning can demonstrate the potential for positive change.

Furthermore, professional development initiatives should be designed to offer gradual, manageable steps rather than overwhelming professors with complex or time-consuming changes. Offering practical training sessions, peer mentoring, and hands-on workshops that allow professors to experiment with new tools and techniques in a supportive environment can ease the transition. Providing ongoing support and emphasizing that professional development is a collaborative process—rather than a top-down mandate—can also help foster a sense of ownership and motivation among faculty members.

Ultimately, for change to be embraced, it is essential that institutions foster a culture that values continuous learning, where professors understand that adapting to new pedagogical approaches and technologies is not just about keeping pace with trends, but about enhancing their effectiveness as educators and improving the overall learning experience for their students.

Financial Constraints Many institutions in Bihar, particularly those in rural or less-developed regions, face significant financial constraints, which limit their ability to invest in faculty training and development programs. With tight budgets, higher education institutions often prioritize basic operational needs such as infrastructure maintenance, salaries, and other essential expenses over professional development opportunities for faculty. This creates a gap in training and development, as faculty members may not have access to the latest tools, teaching methodologies, or research advancements that could enhance their effectiveness in the classroom.

These financial limitations are further exacerbated by the fact that many institutions lack the necessary resources to develop or support in-house training programs or to send faculty members to external workshops, conferences, or seminars. As a result, professors may miss out on valuable opportunities to upgrade their skills, which can impact both the quality of education they provide and their own professional growth.

To mitigate these financial constraints, several strategies can be implemented. Public-private partnerships (PPPs) can be an effective way to pool resources and provide funding for faculty training programs. Collaborations between government bodies, educational institutions, and private sector organizations can help ensure that financial support is available to develop training modules, offer scholarships for faculty development programs, and create infrastructure for online and offline learning.

Additionally, government grants and funding programs can be crucial in supporting faculty development initiatives. Programs like the National Institutional Ranking Framework (NIRF), UGC Faculty Development Scheme, and state-level education grants can be explored by institutions to receive financial assistance for organizing workshops, training sessions, and conferences that benefit faculty members.

Institutional collaboration also plays a significant role in overcoming budget constraints. Partnering with other universities, research institutions, or organizations can help reduce costs while enhancing the scope and quality of faculty development programs. Sharing resources, expertise, and training materials between institutions can create a more cost-effective approach to professional development.

By utilizing these strategies—public-private partnerships, government funding, and inter-institutional collaborations—institutions in Bihar can overcome financial barriers and create an environment conducive to continuous professional development for their faculty, ultimately improving the quality of higher education across the state.

Time Management Balancing the multiple roles of teaching, conducting research, and managing administrative responsibilities presents a significant challenge for professors in higher education, especially in Bihar, where faculty members often juggle a heavy workload. Teaching duties, including preparing lectures, grading, and student interactions, require considerable time and effort. Simultaneously, professors are expected to engage in academic research, publish papers, and contribute to the intellectual community. Additionally, administrative tasks such as committee work, curriculum planning, and institutional development further add to their responsibilities. This combination of tasks often leaves little room for professional development, as time is stretched thin across various obligations.

As a result, many professors struggle to find the time necessary to attend traditional, in-person training programs or professional development sessions, which are often scheduled during work hours or require travel. Consequently, without adequate opportunities for training, professors may fall behind on emerging teaching practices, new technologies, and evolving research methodologies, ultimately affecting their performance and job satisfaction.

To address this time management challenge, flexible, modular, and online training programs present a viable solution. These programs are designed to allow professors to engage in professional development at their own pace, accommodating their busy schedules. By offering on-demand learning modules, asynchronous courses, and bite-sized content, professors can choose when and how they participate in training without interrupting their primary responsibilities. For example, online courses through platforms like SWAYAM, Coursera, or edX can offer a variety of subjects, from digital pedagogy to advanced research methodologies, that professors can complete during their free time or between other tasks.

In addition, modular training programs can be broken down into smaller, manageable sessions, which can be more easily integrated into the professor's routine. These shorter, more targeted learning experiences help professors acquire specific skills or knowledge without committing to long periods of time.

Providing blended learning opportunities, where online content is supplemented by periodic face-to-face interactions, can further enhance the accessibility and flexibility of training. For example, professors could attend online webinars or video lectures for foundational knowledge, followed by practical workshops or collaborative sessions for deeper engagement.

In summary, by offering training opportunities that are flexible, modular, and delivered online, institutions can support faculty members in overcoming time management challenges. This approach allows professors to continually enhance their skills and knowledge base without compromising their existing commitments, ultimately contributing to their professional growth and the overall improvement of teaching quality in higher education.

Conclusion

In conclusion, training for professors in Bihar's higher education sector is a critical component of academic and institutional development. By addressing the evolving needs of the workforce and providing professors with the tools to adapt to a digital and globalized academic environment, Bihar can foster a more engaged, capable, and innovative academic community. Continued investment in faculty development programs, coupled with efforts to overcome challenges such as accessibility and resistance to change, will be pivotal in shaping the future of higher education in the state.